Being Music does the impossibl
improvisation (and the creative p
to be in the libraries of music schc

Ralph Alessi, trumpet player and composer, ECM recording artist,
and faculty, The New School, New York

Mark Miller and Art Lande have been creating music out of thin air
together almost every week for forty years. This thoughtful book
contains many strategies for approaching open improvisation and is
full of lots of insightful gems about the art of music as a life practice.
And it is a lovely chronicle of two special musical artists and their
extraordinary friendship.

Fred Hersch, jazz pianist and composer,
fifteen-time Grammy Award nominee, and
author of *Good Things Happen Slowly: A Life In and Out of Jazz*

Jazz education has long needed additional resources promoting musical
development and its connection to our improvisatory relationship with
life and the present moment. An approach that emphasizes being there
for whatever arises, not altering the music being created around you to
fit personal expectations. An ideology that illustrates how the
realization and acceptance of our own unique gifs is crucial to
supporting and furthering the tradition and rich history of jazz and
improvised music.

Being Music is a much-needed and welcomed addition to musical
literature supporting these goals and will become essential reading for
all those seeking to connect mindfulness and awareness in their daily
lives with how they approach their improvisational and creative
musical endeavors. Highly recommended.

Gary Versace, pianist/keyboardist with John Scofield,
John Abercrombie, Al Foster, Regina Carter,
Maria Schneider, and many others

Mark Miller brings together a long track record of creative artistry, innovative pedagogy and deep contemplative practice in a lively and insightful book. While written from a trans-idiomatic standpoint, the book delineates powerful principles that are relevant to jazz (and other style-based improvisatory formats) as well as stylistically open frameworks. A great complement to the many books that focus on syntax in reflecting on the interior dimensions of the creative process.

Ed Sarath, PhD, Professor of Music, University of Michigan, and author of *Improvisation, Creativity and Consciousness*

In *Being Music*, Mark Miller draws on his decades of experience as both an improvising saxophonist and a teacher–practitioner of mindfulness and meditation. The result is at once a collection of etudes for honing skills in improvisational music and a mini-treatise exploring the philosophical, aesthetic, and even ethical underpinnings of that music. It's a smart, quirky, insightful, provocative, and—best of all—an utterly practical gem of a book.

David Ake, PhD, Chair, Department of Musicology, Frost School of Music, University of Miami, and author of *Jazz Cultures; Jazz Matters: Sound, Place, and Time since Bebop*; and co-editor of the collection *Jazz/Not Jazz: The Music and Its Boundaries*

More than just another book about improvisation, *Being Music* offers a fresh and compelling blueprint for how to build a creative and meaningful life in music. If you've ever felt stuck in a musical rut, obsessed with perfection, insecure about your playing, fearful of uncertainty, or emotionally detached in your music making, Mark Miller and Art Lande are just the teachers to help! Their book is full of musical wisdom, practical insights, creative exercises, and loving encouragement.

Dr. Alex Heitlinger, Professor of Music and Director of Jazz Studies, Collin College

Even the most seasoned improvisers need this book. We all want reminders when it comes to the most essential matters in making music because it's so easy to get distracted by other things, like navigating the economics of the music business. These reminders are like a sip of fresh water or breathing good air, and this book is full of them! *Being Music* will also be a great resource for teachers. Most books on improvisation focus on music theory, but there aren't a lot of books out there that deal with thinking compositionally and that address important topics like roles and relationships in an ensemble, offering tenderness and generosity toward ourselves without an idealized version of the way things are supposed to go in performance.

Rory Cowal, pianist and featured artist: "Best Piano Tracks of 2018," *The New York Times*

I had the privilege of engaging in the practice of "being music" with Mark Miller and Art Lande weekly for many years. Their broad knowledge and experience as musicians, their mastery of the craft of free improvisation, and their openness and generosity as human beings make them perfectly suited to teach other inquisitive souls about this deeply spiritual art form. This book is a gem.

Clare Church, a saxophonist, drummer and educator, has performed with the Joe Henderson Big Band, San Francisco Symphony, Colorado Symphony, Dizzy Gillespie, Benny Carter, Mel Torme, Nancy Wilson, George Shearing, Natalie Cole, and many other jazz and pop artists.

The authors do a fantastic job of describing, in an easy-to-read style, a topic that can be pretty inexplicable. We love how personal it feels, and at the same time how the book manages to give so many great examples of how to hone improvisation skills. We love the "focus on curiosity, not competence," and the de-emphasis on being clever, good, and correct. Best of all, we love the richness of the conversation between these two musicians, so deep after 45 years of working and playing together.

Bonnie Hall, music student

Mark's book provides a profound rescue from the dogmatic traps that formal jazz school often sets for students. He describes an organic approach to improvising that avoids the pitfalls of ego and perfectionism and gets right to the root of what makes improvisation magical. The text skillfully describes how free improvisation can deepen our connection to one another and our relationship to creativity, while shining light on some of the obstacles that keep us from reaching our full ease and potential as music makers. If I could get all of my students to open their minds to the possibilities in improvisation that Mark shows us here, then we'd really be getting somewhere.

Kate Olson, Seattle-based saxophonist, improviser, and educator

The name of this book could easily shorten to its essence—Being. How to be, what it's like when we jump into being in the present moment. Just being with what is occurring, or rather, just being. This is not a static state but dynamically fluid, constantly changing. And there is no solitary, isolated being, but rather what Vietnamese Zen master Thich Nhat Hanh calls "interbeing," the lively dance—responding and expressing—to the world around us and to others who are also dancing in our space. (From the Afterword to *Being Music*).

Judith Simmer-Brown, PhD, Distinguished Professor of Contemplative and Religious Studies at Naropa University, Boulder, Colorado

Being Music
The Art of Open Improvisation

Mark Miller
with
Art Lande

Colorado Springs, CO
www.univeristyprofessorspress.com

Dedication

To Molly, Gabby, Jordan, Krista and Dana
for being who you are.

Table of Contents

Acknowledgments

I am profoundly grateful to my family, friends, and colleagues who have supported me in writing this book. I would especially like to thank my wife, Dana Walker, for her love and critical insight.

Special thanks to Fred Hersch for his straight-ahead and helpful commentary on an early draft, and for his friendly encouragement overall.

Thanks to David Ake, Kent McLagan, Bonnie Hall, Bob Chubrilo, and Rory Cowal for their careful reading and constructive suggestions about early drafts of the book.

Thank you also to Alex Heitlinger, Ed Sarath, Scott Colley, Ralph Alessi, Clare Church, Kate Olson and Gary Versace for their enthusiasm and support.

I am grateful to Naropa University for granting me the sabbatical leave that allowed me to finish this project, and to my colleagues who have contributed so much to my understanding of contemplative mind and practice, including Judith Simmer-Brown, Richard Brown, Dale Asrael, Robert Spellman, Joan Anderson, Regina Smith, Carla Sherrell and all of the faculty, staff, and students of the School of the Arts, including Lorenzo Gonzalez-Fontes, Sue Hammond West, and Liz Acosta. May the sparks forever fly.

Thanks to everyone at University Professors Press, including Louis Hoffman, and especially to Francis Kaklauskas for his patient editing. Without Francis's wholehearted encouragement, this book would not have come to fruition.

Finally, I would like to thank my current family of improvisational co-creators including Khabu Doug Young, Elena Camerin Young, Bill McCrossen, and most especially Art Lande for the musical life we make together.

Foreword

The path of sound creation and spontaneous composition is infinite and profound; a musical pursuit simultaneously simple and complex. Everyone's process and direction on this journey will and should be different. But without a doubt, for every individual, the deeper you dive, the richer the experience.

When I started on this path, it just felt good; it was fun. It still is. But now I see, with some perspective, that it has become inseparable from who I am. The pursuit has enriched my life far beyond what I could have initially imagined. After decades of following the thread, there is no line between *my* music and *my*self. Or if there is a line, I have no idea where it is. That is *being music*.

The search for new sounds and all the possibilities of composition, spontaneous and otherwise, has taught me life lessons. And life has taught me music lessons. All the musicians I've worked with, the personal relationships that have developed, the travels I've experienced, the exposure to other cultures and ways of thought, and lessons of compassion and empathy have all been influenced by music. It has influenced the choices of where I went to school and where I've decided to live. It has helped me work with difficult emotions and taught me to examine the things that make me feel uncomfortable. Spontaneous composition has been a way to look further into the unknown with curiosity and equanimity, rather than prejudice and fear.

Spontaneous composition seems simple, almost ordinary. And at its core, it is. Spontaneous composition is the point of departure for the music I create. It's the starting point of all sounds, textures, grooves and includes all ideas that mature into written compositions. I begin with a sound from my instrument, or from others in the group. When I am drawn to a sound, I make decisions on how to respond. Then others make sound, and I respond to that—or not. There is a gravitational pull that directs the decisionmaking, including aesthetic, emotional, and physical components. And, of course, the central element of making music with others is empathy, similar to any meaningful conversation. From there we move as a group into considerations of theme and development, transforming sound-making into story. As we work our way forward, we see that the music deepens and becomes more complicated. Then gravity takes over again and simplicity returns.

"Why do I make music?" One answer is that music is a language that has the potential to connect me to all humanity in a meaningful way—a much more meaningful language for me than any other I possess. This has remained paramount over time. As long as I'm listening, the music created can be a conversation. It can be both statement and question. By placing myself at the center of these conversations, I am also taking on the challenge of responding to all that is around me with the most honesty and consciousness that I am capable of at that moment.

Regardless of where you are, or think you are, on your musical journey, *Being Music* is a beautiful and insightful book. It presents or reminds us in a very organized and poetic way of the possibilities and 'tools 'available to us as spontaneous composers/musicians/seekers. It has become routine for many of us in our modern world to become fragmented by technology and information. There is a tendency to compare and a push to succeed. Mark and Art guide us away from those patterns of thinking and toward a place of greater wonder and discovery.

This book very clearly presents the questions vital for each individual and ensemble to ask and presents possibilities and exercises that point one in the direction of finding answers—each individual's unique answers. The exploration of sound is the vehicle that brings us awareness of the present moment. It is a way to bring about greater understanding of our perceived consciousness and our relationships. As Mark says, "Our business is to be present."

For those exploring spontaneous composition for the first time, this book is an incredible and unpretentious journey. And, for those of us who have made it our life's work to pursue this path, *Being Music* is a beautiful reminder of the vital role music has in making sense of our individual experience and relationships. Let this book take you into a deep view of this process with two masters.

Scott Colley
June 23, 2020

Scott Colley has been called "one of the leading bassists of our postbop era, and a composer–bandleader of quietly serious resolve" (*The New York Times*) and "one of the most musical bassists playing today [with a] natural, intuitive, empathic sense of how to bring the most out of the other musicians and the music he's playing" (Joshua Redman.) Renowned for his role in groups led by headliners Carmen McRae, Andrew Hill, Jim Hall, John Scofield, Herbie Hancock, Chris Potter, Michael Brecker, and many others, Colley is a is four-time Grammy nominee who has performed on over 200 recordings, eight as composer and leader.

Introduction

"This isn't real music. They're just making it up."

Sometime during the early 1970s, my friend Cookie Marenco[1] invited me to listen to a new band she was excited about. "You won't believe it; they're really *out there*," she said. I was intrigued, so we drove north over the Golden Gate Bridge to the little town of Cotati and The Inn of the Beginning, a rustic rock n' roll venue in Sonoma County. As we walked into the club, Art Lande was sitting at an upright piano reading a story about a bird and a mountain. Trumpeter Mark Isham played the bird, while the rest of the band (The Rubisa Patrol) created the sounds of the mountain environment, improvising with a sweet soulfulness that captivated the room.

I had been studying jazz theory and history and was trying to master the idiom. I wanted to know how the musicians thought about what they were doing.

"What about scales and modes? Was there a chord progression?"

"No... we just play what we hear," said Art.

"But how do you justify the notes you play? You mean *anything* is possible?"

"Pretty much...."

Improvisation is an awareness practice, meaning that we rely on our own experience more than on a composer's notes on a page. When a musical idea arises in the imagination or a rhythm is born in the body,

---

[1] Cookie Marenco is a Grammy-nominated producer, recording engineer, and founder of Blue Coast Records.

we play it. Improvisation is about creative agency and musical community. For some of us, it doesn't get more "real" than that.

Improvised music emerges from stillness and evolves organically as an investigation of individual and group creativity. Improvisation is a disciplined response to a unique set of musical circumstances requiring absolute fidelity to the present moment in body and mind. This fidelity, or presence, incorporates all aspects of our human experience, including sense perception, emotion, imagination, and the spaciousness of listening and not doing. In improvisation, we play who we are.

Conceptual understanding is also important. If the music is in a minor key, music theory suggests a number of options that I might employ in response—minor scales, pentatonic scales, modes, chromaticism, and arpeggiation, to name a few. But the intellect doesn't know what to make of these options; it can only point to them. The creative process of improvisation is fundamentally intuitive, arising out of presence, not thinking alone.

A central topic of this book is open improvisation, a form of spontaneous music making with no pre-arranged content or form. Since the 1960s, some have called this approach "free jazz" or "free music," but, as our friend and colleague Jerry Granelli emphatically asks, "Oh yeah? Free from what?"

In open improvisation, all of the elements of music are available to us including melody, harmony, meter, rhythm, groove, texture, feel, dynamics, counterpoint, motion, stillness, and form. We call this approach "spontaneous composition," and spontaneous composers are bound by the same constraints as any other composer. We seek clarity, authenticity and economy of means in what we create. Ideally, the only difference between improvised and composed music is that the former isn't written down.

In the book, we also consider structured forms of improvisation, including jazz. Freedom and form occupy different poles of a creative continuum, and we investigate how both inspire and shape the music we play.

Art Lande and I have played music together for over 45 years. Our kids grew up together; Art is my daughter Jordan's godfather. Although I have written and edited the text of *Being Music*, the ideas presented here are sourced in our combined playing experience and in the countless conversations we've had about improvisation—what it is and how to do it.

Interspersed throughout the book are transcriptions of dialogs that we recorded in 2018 and 2019 as we looked back at our long playing careers. This commentary (mostly by Art) appears in *italics*. Also included are practical exercises and written musical examples.

Art is one of the most versatile and skilled improvisers on the planet. He has performed and recorded with some of the top jazz musicians of the modern era including Joe Henderson, Bobby Hutcherson, Steve Swallow, Kenny Wheeler, Woody Shaw, Sheila Jordan, Jan Garbarek and many others. You can find his full discography at artlande.com. My discography and our duo recordings are available on my website: markmillermusic.net.

Many of the skills and personal capacities necessary for effective improvisation are cultivated in traditional mindfulness/awareness practices such as meditation, tai chi, aikido, ikebana, and yoga. These capacities include openness, courage, generosity, and a willingness to serve the greater good of our musical community. We include perspectives from Zen Buddhism, as well as those of other mindfulness traditions and teachers as a framework for understanding some of the principles and practices of improvisation.

In meditation and in improvisation, we practice being present with whatever happens while recognizing that reality, and our thoughts and feelings about reality, are not the same thing. This is an important distinction for musicians. When we play music, we immerse ourselves in the world of sound and the quickly changing flow of melody, harmony, and rhythm, and we notice that we have thoughts and feelings about all of that, which is a very different level of experience. The meditation teacher and scholar Judith Simmer-Brown (1998) says that meditation is "a technology that allows us to perceive the difference between thinking and being." Likewise, in improvisation we can learn to recognize the difference between thinking about music and *being music.*

Art doesn't meditate—he says he doesn't know how—but I draw on many years of Zen practice and decades of teaching at Naropa University, a leader in the contemporary mindfulness movement. I am indebted to the many extraordinary teachers and colleagues I have encountered at Naropa, including Kobun Chino Otogawa Roshi, Roshi Bernie Glassman, Roshi Sandra Jishu Holmes, Acharya Judith Simmer-Brown, and Rabbi Zalman Schachter-Shalomi. I took lay ordination (*jukai*)) in the Zen Peacemaker Order in 1998 with Bernie Glassman and Jishu Holmes. My study and practice of Zen meditation continues to inform and enrich my life as an improviser.

We hope you enjoy this exploration of spontaneous music making—what it is, and how to do it.

Mark Miller
Boulder, Colorado
January 2020

Chapter 1

Being Music

On a train at the airport, the afternoon sun flickers across the faces of the passengers like a scene from a silent movie. Oblivious to the sights and sounds of the rolling train car, my fellow travelers focus their attention on their digital devices. Some trail ear buds; others wear headphones like Micky Mouse ears. Their objective is to escape the everyday reality of wheeled suitcases, crying children in Hello Kitty backpacks, security warnings, and gate change announcements. They want to filter out the "real" world, find a better view on their phones, listen to a better soundtrack, attenuate the cacophony of San Francisco International Airport. Later, people stand in line at the BART station, still staring at their little screens. No one notices the afternoon slipping into evening, the darkening sky, the clattering train as it recedes into the tunnel.

> Because I know that time is always time
> And place is always and only place
> And what is actual is actual only for one time
> And only for one place
> I rejoice that things are as they are
> —T.S. Eliot "Ash Wednesday" (1967)

Improvisation is a practice of exploration and discovery. What we explore is our "actual" experience, and what we discover we share with our audience.

"Just play what's on your inner radio," as Art likes to say. We play sensation and imagination: a rhythm, a few notes of melody, a texture, a sound, a feeling or emotion. In improvisation, we play the life we're living.

Art: We are being as music. We are transforming our being into the sound of our being, and there's nobility in that, there's beauty in that, and there's integrity in that. I think it's the same for painters or poets: How do I share my flow, my being, as part of the world?

In teaching, I start from humanity, rather than music. I'd been teaching at the School for Improvisational Music in New York. The students had spent four days in this miraculous city, and they'd never been around so many people who made music really full-on. I asked them, "What have you noticed this week, or what was new for you to discover in yourself?" And that opened up some good things and made us all the same, in a way.

I look for ways of sharing that eliminate the question, "Am I good? Are they better than me?" We have impulses and we sense each other and we can make music together. We start without instruments, with movement, language, and drawing; then the instruments can express the basic things that we're seeing, feeling, sensing, and hearing without asking, "Am I good?" The instruments are amplifiers of our bodies, minds, and spirits. Their value is to take our inner world and let it out. Otherwise, the music is about our technical prowess rather than an expression of inner seeing.

So much music is available to us through Spotify, iTunes, YouTube, and live performance that we live in a "post stylistic" era when no single genre or musical aesthetic predominates. We can listen to almost anything from any place and time, from noise to North African and South Indian music, from hip-hop and punk to classical and jazz. The good news is that we can access whatever music we want. The "bad news" is that we have to sort through a bewildering array of influences to find out who we are and how we fit in as musicians.

Some improvisers find that they fit comfortably within a particular idiom like bebop or the blues. They enjoy improvising within a traditional form and find that structure offers a source of collective inspiration and direction. Other musicians are most inspired by the challenges of open improvisation, an investigation of musical possibility free from prearranged content or form.

In either case, we begin with stillness, a momentary reset, one deep breath before the first note sounds. We begin by letting go of fixed ideas and opinions about the music. We begin by paying attention.

Improvisation is a mindfulness/awareness practice, a meditation on sound and creative expression in community with other musicians and the audience. Mindfulness is "paying attention to what's happening while it's happening" (Grossenbacher, 2012) and awareness is our ability to see the big picture, the larger context of what we're about. You don't need to practice meditation in order to improvise, but it's important to find a way to cultivate the qualities of mindfulness and awareness: to be open, awake and ready to join in.

Chapter 2

Creative Resources

I often find that having an idea in my head prevents me from doing something else. Working is therefore a way of getting rid of an idea.
  —Jasper Johns (2010)

Ideas? Oh man, I got a million dreams. That's all I do—I dream. All the time. This isn't piano, this is dreaming.
  —Duke Ellington (2013)

To be creative, I occupy the present moment in body and mind and I share my experience with others. I don't worry about right or wrong, good or bad; I don't hold the music hostage to my ideas about success or failure. Improvised music is an expression of who we are— physically, emotionally, conceptually, in spirit and imagination. These are our creative resources.

Art: We want to allow in all the parts of being human: physical, emotional, conceptual... and I don't like the word "spiritual" that much, but I don't know how else to put it. What if I use the top and the bottom notes so that I can hug all the sounds in between? That would be a spiritual way of joining. I'm going to go wider than I usually go and see if that encompasses everything. To me, that's not a thought; it's a spirit wish.

Some people only think and play, or they play only from muscle memory. Some avoid playing from feeling because they don't know what they feel, or they don't understand their basic energy: "Who am I? What do I have to offer?"

> The most important question you can ask is, "What is it that you truly love? What is it that makes you, you?"
> –Dame Evelyn Glennie (Riedelsheimer, 2006)

Exercise: You Playing You

In this five-part exercise, you can investigate any section that interests you, or you can play the sections in order as a suite. Take your time. Enjoy the investigation.

First, let your body play. Move with your instrument in a way that pleases you and play the sound of your dancing. Then play how you feel: your delight, sadness, excitement, or calm. Next play from a thought or concept. For example, play a piece based on a pattern of five notes, then four notes, then two, or a piece using a familiar scale or mode. Then explore your imagination: play a willow tree beside a still pond. Add some ducks. Finally, play the energy that animates and inspires you. Play you.

Listening

One of our most important creative resources is sense perception— what we see, hear, smell, taste, and touch. Of course, for musicians, the most important of these is listening.

> You are now listening to me; you are not making an effort to pay attention, you are just listening; and if there is truth in what you hear, you will find a remarkable change taking place in you—a change that is not premeditated or wished for, a transformation, a complete revolution in which the truth alone is master and not the creations of your mind. And if I may suggest it, you should listen in

that way to everything—not only to what I am saying, but also to what other people are saying, to the birds, to the whistle of the locomotive, to the noise of the bus going by. You will find that the more you listen to everything, the greater is the silence, and that silence is then not broken by noise. It is only when you are resisting something, when you are putting up a barrier between yourself and that to which you do not want to listen—it is   only then that there is a struggle. (Krishnamurti, 1995)

At a meditation retreat, I heard Zen master Kobun Chino Otogawa Roshi (1999) give this instruction to his students: "All you have to do is sit and listen to the dharma." Since *dharma* is a word that can mean "the truth of the world as it is," I thought this the perfect instruction for a musician like me. All I have to do is listen to the world around me. At the retreat, I began to focus my attention on listening, and the world seemed changed.

Art: As Mark plays, I sing it inside me. I AM it, rather than merely hearing it. I call this "listening at source." The music is in me rather than "over there."

Listening allows us to interact with the world and with one another free from conceptual mediation. Careful listening orients us in the present moment, allowing us to make music that feels natural and true. Listening is an open invitation, a way of touching and being touched.

Art: When my kids were babies and would cry, if I could make the same sounds they made, they would stop and stare at me. If you hear a grating or annoying sound and you can be it, it dissolves into you. If there is no subject/object, if you are the world, the world cannot victimize you; you are not its effect.

To listen is to open without resistance or expectation. In the Zen Peacemaker Order (2019), this opening practice is called *not knowing.*

Not knowing is defined as "entering a situation without being attached to any opinion, idea, or concept. This means total openness, deep listening to the situation."

> We used to talk about it as "playing music as if you've never heard music before."
> —Charlie Haden (Burns, 2001a)

Exercise: Symphony of Place
(from *The Listening Book*, by W.A. Mathieu, 1991)

Get a pencil and paper. Become aware of all the sounds you are hearing now, this moment, as you read. Make a list of them, Close your eyes from time to time. Swivel your head slightly to change the mix. Make a sweep from nearby sounds to distant sounds. Fall into the distance. Become transparent. Now fall into the nearness. Make a sweep from the highest sounds to the lowest ones.

Now make your sweeps into scans so rapid that you have the illusion of hearing everything at once. Now close your eyes and hear everything at once. Now cup your hands behind your ears. Technicolor!

Normally when we listen, we label sounds as they enter our awareness (if we hear them at all.) I play a note on the piano. I recognize that sound; I've heard it before. I name it: concert A above middle C. By labeling the sound, I assert that I "know" it, and once we think we know something, we unconsciously assume that there is little left to learn or appreciate about it.

Art: Our education system fails to honor our instinctive animal selves by being so focused on naming and spelling. As a preschool teacher, I realized that my real job was to let the children retain their sense of an "eraser" as something special: a pink, chewy, bendable, bounce-able, fragrant thing, a thing beyond its grownup function and name that reduces it to, "just an eraser, silly!" It's no longer an "ewaso," with cool sensual qualities that need to be explored. Our education system does this so we can be socialized, rather than wild. If we all know that this is just a pencil and here's how you use it, then there's no play anymore. It doesn't have a smell and a taste. You can't use it as a percussion instrument.

By listening without labeling, by practicing not knowing, we free ourselves to learn more about the world around us, and to appreciate "things as it is," as Zen master Shunryu Suzuki Roshi (2012) put it. Suzuki (1970) called this freedom "beginners mind" (p. 21). Listening opens our beginner's mind. Listening is our primary practice.

There are many kinds of thinking, and listening is not any of them.
—W.A. Mathieu (1991)

Exercise: Ear Walk

Go for a walk. Try to match the sounds that you hear with your voice, or by clapping or playing your body. Otherwise be silent. Match the sounds of the world as they happen rather than by imitating them afterward. Match their texture and volume: birds, cars, wind, planes, insects, radios, horns, conversations, doors closing, sirens, a river, workmen pounding. Hear the world and be the world.

Exercise: Ear Talk

Sit quietly with a partner somewhere you won't be disturbed. Turn off your phone. Listen, and then list the sounds you hear on a piece of paper. If you can't identify a sound, include it on your list by describing it as best you can. After about ten minutes, face your partner and engage in a dialog using only the sounds on your lists. Reproduce the sounds with your voice and body as accurately as you can (don't just describe them or name them.) Be expressive. Have a meaningful conversation using only ear talk.

Art: It's hard for people to play and hear because they're so focused on being good at what they're doing. It's difficult to be open when you're trying really hard rather than trusting. You rob yourself of the reason for the music, which is to hear something! It's like, "I don't have the luxury of listening to the other people. I've got to play these sixteenth notes, and I have to work really hard to be able to do it. Therefore, I don't receive anything, including music itself, because it's all in this effort of competence or mastery. Focus on curiosity, not competence. Effortless mystery!

Working with Emotion

According to psychologist John Welwood (1979), our emotions manifest on a spectrum from simple well-being to the mosaic of thoughts and feelings that describe our complex relationships with friends and family. Strong emotions like anger or jealousy can hijack our awareness and challenge our ability to respond skillfully to a difficult life situation. Welwood notes that we tend to think of emotion as something separate from ourselves, something that happens *to* us. But emotion is part of who we are, part of the richness of human experience. As such, emotional energy is a creative resource.

Exercise: Instant Opera

With its dramatic text, colorful costumes, and bel canto singing, opera is especially effective at expressing emotion through music. Opera encompasses the passions of larger-than-life characters in romantic turmoil or existential crisis, but music can also express the emotional content of everyday life, giving voice to what moves us while creating community through our shared experience.

Take a few minutes and write a short description of a life situation that has some emotional charge for you. It could be an incident from your childhood or a more recent event. It could be funny or sad, joyful or tragic, significant or trivial, but choose a story that has an emotional quality of some kind. A story that you would like to share with others (not just, "I did the laundry and then I washed the car.")

Once you've written your story, read it aloud, delivering just the facts of your experience. Now sing or play the underlying emotional quality of your story. Don't worry about technique; focus on the feeling and on the emotional content and meaning of your story. This is your instant opera.

My story: When I was a child, I lived next door to my friend Kathy Burroughs, a spunky eight-year-old girl with whom I shared a passion for baseball cards and marbles. One sunny afternoon I wanted to impress Kathy, so I climbed the fence that separated my front and back yards. Balancing like a tightrope walker, I began to feel my way along the two-by-four frame at the top of the fence. This stunt ended dramatically when Kathy opened the gate under my feet and I crashed, headfirst, onto the brick walkway below. I broke my collarbone and, vomiting and delirious, spent the night in the hospital with a concussion. Kathy was not impressed.

From a child's perspective, this tale has elements of fear, sadness, embarrassment, and pain. From my grownup perspective, it also has humor and irony. As I play the story on my instrument, the music will have meaning and purpose to the extent that I embody and communicate its emotional richness as I play. Emotion is one of our most important creative resources.

Working with the Imagination

Art: Improvisation is easy. Just play what you want to hear, and when you don't want it anymore, stop.

If you could play anything, any kind of music, what would you play? What do you want to listen to? What do you need to hear right now? One way to approach improvisation is to use your imagination as a portal into a world that you create as you play. You can enter the portal whenever you want and go wherever you want to go. All you need is your imagination and a willingness to travel.

The goal isn't to produce an exact replica of your imagined world. I can imagine the sound of a symphony orchestra, but I can't duplicate that with my flute. I can, however, play with the sonorous richness and romantic passion of my dream orchestra. I can capture the essence of a cello line on my bass flute or sketch an imagined melody with my soprano saxophone. Even if I can't play the exact notes, I can realize the basic shape and phrasing of my melody; I can play the atmosphere of a distant moon; I can party with the energy of an imagined rhythmic groove. With practice, we can develop more precision with pitch and rhythm and become more articulate in manifesting imaginary worlds.

Exercise: Sing and Play

Sing something. Keep it simple; two or three notes will suffice in the beginning. Then play what you sang. If you can't reproduce the tones precisely, make adjustments on your instrument until you can play exactly what you heard. When you find a series of tones you like, learn it in all 12 keys (be able to play your melody starting on any note on your instrument.)

Variation 1: If you know solfeggio or are familiar with numbering the notes of a scale, sing a simple pattern (do, sol, sol, do, re, or 1, 5, 5, 1, 2) and then play the pattern on your instrument in all 12 keys.

Variation 2: Sing a melody and then play its shape and rhythm *without* precisely duplicating the notes; play a rough sketch of your melody. Do the best you can. In performance, we often work this way, playing a gesture rather than an exact replica of what we imagine note for note.

Imagination is a place to start—a suggestion, not a blueprint. Play what you want to hear as best you can, but don't be too fussy. Be willing to work with imperfection. Keep in mind that what you played might sound even better than what you imagined, or that a misshapen melody can turn the music in a surprising but interesting new direction. In improvisation, we need to stay open to possibility, to listen, and not be too attached to our creative dreaming.

Guided Meditation: Imaginary Music

After you read this, get comfortable. Lie on the floor or go outside and lie in the grass. Close your eyes. Breathe. Take time to relax and rest. Imagine that you and I are on our way to a concert. We have plenty of time, so we stop for dinner at my favorite restaurant. The atmosphere here is warm and friendly and the food is uncommonly good. In fact, this is unlike any restaurant you've ever been to. Any dish you dream up, you can have—any culinary style from anywhere in the world. The food is fresh and expertly prepared.

When our food arrives, we take pleasure in the sensual feast, the union of fragrance, texture, and flavor. We savor each bite and finish our meal with gratitude and appreciation for the chef.

After a short walk to the concert hall, we find our seats as the house lights dim and the musicians take their places. We smile as we settle in, recognizing that one of the performers onstage is you! The crowd quiets and the concert begins. Listen...what do you hear? What are you playing? You can play whatever you want to hear.

For a few minutes, relax and enjoy the music. Then open your eyes, go to your instrument and play (or sing) what you imagined, remembering that you don't have to transcribe your performance note for note. Inhabit your imagined world without worrying too much about capturing its details. Use your imagination as a source of inspiration or creative direction. You might also pick up a musical idea or two—a melodic line or a rhythm—but don't worry if you can't play it exactly. Imagination is a place to start, a resource, but the sounding world is where we do our work.

Chapter 3

Sharing Your Story

There is a vitality, a life force, an energy, a quickening that is translated through you into action, and because there is only one of you in all of time, this expression is unique. And if you block it, it will never exist through any other medium and it will be lost. The world will not have it. It is not your business to determine how good it is nor how valuable nor how it compares with other expressions. It is your business to keep it yours clearly and directly, to keep the channel open. You do not even have to believe in yourself or your work. You have to keep yourself open   and aware to the urges that motivate you. Keep the channel open.
— Martha Graham (as cited in de Mille, 1991, p. 264)

As an undergraduate, I studied music theory with Sister Anne Cecile Daigle, a Catholic nun, composer, and former student of Paul Hindemith. Sister Anne Cecile had little patience for what she considered the watered-down music of Vatican II: the three-chord folk songs that had supplanted "serious music" in the Catholic mass. She was an adventurous composer and a dedicated teacher with a kind heart and somewhat intimidating bearing. When I handed her my homework, she sometimes said in her sisterly way, "This is very good, but it's not quite *wonderful*," or, "We already have this." She meant that what I had written was competent, but there wasn't enough *me* in it. I hadn't yet found my voice.

When we learn to play music, especially when we learn in school or in college, we spend most of our time studying "the tradition"—the repertoire, history, theory, and vocabulary of jazz or classical music. This canon is what worked in the past, what W.A. Mathieu (1992) calls the scar of music—what's left behind after the music is gone. But music is more than "what's left behind." Music is also an expression of who we are, here and now. To make music, we have to tell our own story.

Art: Everybody has stories. People's lives are stories. A lot of pieces I write are about places, people, or events that happened in my life that I can share without words. Just as when we improvise there can be a succession of things that feel like a story—this happens, and then that happens; the whole thing makes a story.

It's personal but it's also not so personal. It can be, "I saw the ocean and the ocean is amazing. I want to honor the ocean even though it's only my point of view about the ocean. I want to bring people to the ocean through the music." What is it like to listen to birds? What is it like to be in a city? I can't bring everybody to Miami, but I can play a piece that comes out of my time in Miami that gives the vitality of that experience.

Mark: It's also about who we are as a community, not just my personal experience.

Art: Exactly. So, it's a group communication of a story, or of an aesthetic, or something that we're interested in.

Mark: Sometimes people are afraid to tell the story of who they are.

Art: Well, they think their story isn't worthy, or they're ashamed, or they're embarrassed about how well they can tell it. But when a person isn't telling a clear story in music or in words, what you get is, "Oh, I'm hungry. Where's the dog? When do I have to leave on this trip? How is my team doing? Where did I leave my book? How's Mom? My left foot hurts." It's honest, in a way, but that's not how I live.

I love focus. I love being part of a linear story. Not that there can't be non sequiturs or collages, but for me most of life is "this follows that" and that makes it engaging. If the music is just random synapses firing, my heart doesn't open. I can't invest in anything. Who is my character? Who do I love? Who's dying? The story involves themes and ideas that return.

I asked Tara Boyle, who teaches music theory at Portland State University, if she were able to analyze our music, and she said, "No, all I can say is that you use repetition." She said that we can't really understand music without some sense of repetition, whether it's a tone you come back to, or a rhythm, or something that stays throughout. Just like in a story, there's a character who is in both scenes rather than all new characters in all new situations. I think it's natural to bond with something specific.

Exercise: Two Lists

In this exercise, we tell the story of a chosen musical topic or characteristic. Just as in composed music, an improvised piece often has a primary focus, something we can bond with and explore with our friends.

First, make a list of everything you know how to play on your instrument, both conventional and non-conventional. Of course, this list is endless, so for now, limit yourself to 25 things.

Technical/Musical List
Staccato (short notes)
legato (smoothly connected notes)
minor scales
major scales
modes
arpeggios
the blues
swing rhythms
funk rhythms
long tones
breathy tones
pure tones

high notes
low notes
loud notes
soft notes
bent notes
repeating notes
tonality (playing within a key)
atonality (playing outside of a key)
ascending lines
descending lines
playing in time (with a rhythmic pulse)
playing out of time (no rhythmic pulse)
playing in time out of time (from Charlie Haden—relating to the
    pulse but not playing it literally. The pianist Fred Hersch calls
    this, "emotional rhythm.")

Now make a second list, a life list. Include anything in life that you can express musically (that's just about everything).

Life List

lazy	grey sky
unpredictable	silly
bouncy	shaky
cold	sneaky
round	empty
angular	joyful
scary	mournful
a forest	the ocean
boring	my brain

Anything from either of your lists could serve as the focus of an improvised piece. Choose one item from each list and create a short improvisation based solely on those elements. The first list represents the musical or technical focus of your piece, the second list describes its feel or character. The key is to choose something alive, something interesting to you. Or let the piece choose you: What sparks your imagination? What calls to you? Which elements want or need to be translated into sound?

The topics needn't be so literal that they become clichés. For example, each time I play the feeling of gratitude it comes out differently. One day the feeling is joyous, another day it has a bit of humility in it. Or irony. A piece about low notes could be loud and fast one day, staccato and dancy the next. Within "low," much can happen. What is the nature of low? How low is low? How low can you go?

Drawing on my lists, I begin with a series of mournful long tones. I've chosen these elements because I'm intrigued by them, not because they're special, not because they're particularly creative or innovative, but because these are the elements that are alive for me right now. The materials I choose to work with might be humble, but because they spark my interest or trigger something in my imagination, that's what I play.

The success of my piece will depend on the quality and depth of my commitment to exploration and discovery. To explore is to drop deeply into a specific area of interest and investigate its character and substance. Imagine exploring a country you've never visited before. Are you by the sea or in the mountains? Are there trees, rocks, exotic birds? How's the weather? The opposite of conscious exploration is unconscious experimentation, trying a little of this and a little of that with no real interest or commitment. A haphazard approach to improvisation—because you don't yet know what you truly want to explore—yields an unfocused and arbitrary music.

Art: I don't like "messing around." I don't like that form. When the music doesn't have a degree of elucidation or form, then I can't bond with it. I don't know what I'm doing. I don't know what I'm a part of or serving.

I think improvisation is about worlds that you visit in your imagination and that you play. I like these tones and that rhythm because they brought me peacefulness, or they brought me mystery, and I want to share that with the audience.

First Thought, Best Thought

Many Zen traditions teach that simplicity is key—the simplicity of working with whatever arises in the moment. We run into trouble when we're too choosey, rejecting spontaneity in favor of some hoped-for greatness that we think is just around the corner. In improvisation, we don't have time to pick and choose, we work with what we're given.

"First thought, best thought" was how Tibetan meditation master and scholar Chögyam Trungpa (1991) described this principle. When a creative impulse arises, we go with that. We don't waste time on evaluation and internal debate; we don't wait for certainty, for something "good" or "great" or "better" to come along. The only certainty in improvisation is the "ordinary magic" of our immediate experience.

Art: I remember playing a free piece with a student and we got to a place where he just shut down. I asked what happened and he said, "I heard five different things, and I didn't know which one to choose. How do you do it?" I told him that I don't get to five. I do the first one. Even if I don't play it and I hold it, I'm not picking between five options at all. The first one that you hear is fine. Don't give in to self-doubt, that what you imagined wasn't good enough because it wasn't special, or wasn't right, or you think you don't know how to play it.

The principle of first thought, best thought is not absolute. One consideration is timing. I might imagine something wonderful to play, but my creative idea might better serve the music if I were to wait until the piece really needs what I have to offer. A second consideration is context. What is alive for me might be too lively for others in that moment, too disruptive or unsuitable for the music we're playing. With awareness, I can balance impulse, timing, and context as the piece unfolds.

Art: You might realize that the thing you imagine playing won't communicate what you mean at that moment. I hear the thing, but I might choose not to play it because it's not the right time, or maybe the piece doesn't need that. When the idea is hot, like when you're thinking, "This music is kind of boring, I'm going to make a big noise," maybe you're not being patient enough. If something comes up and you don't see the way or the time to play it, then leave it out. If the baby is sleeping and I think about playing some music for them, I'll wait until they wake up. The piece is our baby; the question is, how do we nourish them?

Musical habits can be problematic also—habits of too much exposure or too little, habits of intrusiveness or weirdness. Some people are habitually too conservative; they never express what they sense. Habits can be neurotic and block our being. You have to know yourself well enough to get past those kinds of habits, to realize when it's good to let the music out, or when it's good to let it out softer so it can merge with the others without blowing the whole thing to bits. These are things we practice every day.

Mark: So, we're confronted with a paradox, which seems to happen a lot when we talk about improvisation. We play whatever comes up in the moment, but not always?

Art: Well, most things you just play. I like the idea that the music or the life is wide enough that the piece can expand, that it can include whatever you need to say. If what you play is always "appropriate," then the music will lack spaciousness or authentic relationship. Sometimes I have to slam a drawer, even if it wakes the baby. Is there room for me to slam a drawer without it being the end of the world, or taken as disrespect?

The Piece, the Self and the Other

Art: I think of this as a three-part system: the piece, the self, and the other. You care about each person in the band, including yourself, and therefore the piece can expand. Remember when Mark Isham[1] started taking 45-minute solos with the Rubisa Patrol?[2] He was intrigued by Coltrane and wanted to see if he could develop his solo over a long period. Some people didn't like it, but we supported him because it was an honest inquiry; he was trying to learn how to do that.

The inquiry might even hurt the piece or make it too long, but we're learning and growing and supporting one another. We ask the audience to support it, too. But if they can't, they can leave. Or I can leave, or I can butt in, or I can do whatever I want. But I value the spaciousness of allowing things that are not always totally perfect or right, so that it doesn't get too prissy with everybody tiptoeing around, doing the perfect thing all the time, always following the rules.

We need to acknowledge that it's okay to sense it and do it, not only because it fits the piece, but because you need to do it, and we're supportive of your personal growth. That's the love of each person, including the audience. Instead of judging, ask, "What are they up to?" Maybe you think they're not doing that great, but wait a couple of months, come back and listen, and then see what you think.

---

[1] Mark Isham is a trumpet player and award-winning TV and film composer whose works include *Never Cry Wolf, Crash, Black Mirror, Fame, The Times of Harvey Milk, A River Runs Through It,* and hundreds more.
[2] Rubisa Patrol was a seminal improvisational ensemble from the San Francisco Bay Area. Their recordings are available on ECM records.

Chapter 4

Flow

Art has always been about devotion to the unknown.
    —Joan Anderson (2020)

In improvisation we seek experience and insight into an area of musical investigation. When we surrender fully to the inquiry, we're in flow, a state of oneness and complete absorption called *samadhi* in Buddhism and Hinduism. Flow happens when we pay attention. Flow happens when we're present and available, and when we respond without overthinking.

Csikszentmihalyi (1991) describes flow as an optimal experience in which

> Concentration is so intense that there is no attention left over to think about anything irrelevant, or to worry about problems. Self-consciousness disappears and the sense of time becomes distorted. An activity that produces such experience is so gratifying that people are willing to do it for its own sake, with little concern for what they will get out of it, even when it is difficult, or dangerous. (p. 71)

Flow is not about technical perfection. You don't have to be a virtuoso to experience flow; just refrain from doing anything that interrupts the flow. Flow is inhibited by a lack of commitment, by reluctance and indecision. Flow is negated when we make creative choices out of pride or insecurity. We lose track of flow when we are overly concerned about outcome. When we make choices based on our devotion to the music, our creative curiosity, and our support of the other musicians, we can be in flow.

> So [it] doesn't matter what kind of work you are doing as an artist. The most important [thing] is from which state of mind you are doing what you are doing. Performance is all about state of mind.
> —Marina Abramović (Akers, 2012)

In improvisation, flow happens when we abandon any thought of how the music is *supposed* to go, any idea of what should or shouldn't happen, and instead direct our attention to what is. Flow is our natural state unconditioned by our preferences and opinions. Flow is always available to us. The question is, how available are we to let go and dive in?

Art: We just want to let the music play. It isn't ours. We don't own it. When the source says "Play dit-a-dut, dit-a-dut," I do it, even if it's weirdly against what's going on in the music. I'm not doing it to give you a problem. I'm doing it because that's the transmission from source, which I trust because I don't know what else to listen to. This is the connection with the so-called spiritual, how you live. The music is always playing; you can hear it and let it out. It's in the air or in the room. It exists.

To be in flow, allow yourself to be guided by awareness, by your imagination and embodied presence. The opposite approach is to construct a performance according to a conceptual model of how you think the music *should* go. Our experience of flow depends on our orientation, playing either from awareness or from a conceptual model.

Awareness	**Conceptual Model**
openness	right/wrong thinking
welcoming	comparing
willingness to explore	aversion to risk
embracing what happens	fear of losing control
equanimity	judgment
selflessness	self-centeredness
lightness, freedom	tightness, constriction
focus on process	focus on outcome
curiosity and delight	perfectionism, self-doubt
trust in others	wanting to control others
hearing, receiving the music	forgetting to listen
spaciousness, breathing	fear of space, cluttering

It's about forgetting things and letting the subconscious take over…. You can't think and play at the same time. I've tried it—can't do it. You just have to put yourself in the state of mind where there's no conscious thought. And then let the music come out.
— Sonny Rollins (2016)

Art: I once went to shoot hoops at the park with one of my sons. He was just a kid, but he was on fire, making every shot, and I kept saying— too many times— "Amazing!" or "That's great!" And then he started missing everything. Later he said, "Papa, you kind of ruined it." And I said, "What did I do? I was just enjoying it." And he said, "Yeah, but the more you said how good it was, the more I kept trying to be that good, and then I couldn't."

Mark: Our business is to be present, not to be "good."

Art: Our business is to do what we're doing and have it be how it really is. It's good when it's fragmented; it's good when it's shy; it's good because it's authentic. It's not about what we produce, and it's not about getting acknowledgement. It's about natural flow.

Judgment vs. Discernment

We can't control flow. We can, however, interfere with it. The quickest way to get tossed out of flow onto the rocks of disappointment is to engage in judgmental thinking while we're trying to play.

Because judgment interrupts the flow of the music, binary thinking that results in good/bad or right/wrong messages is unhelpful. Instead of judging, I simply notice what works and what needs more attention. By practicing awareness, we can relax the closed fist of hard judgment and play with compassion for ourselves and others.

This doesn't mean that we never think critically about what we play. Critical evaluation has its place and time, but that place and time is after we play, while we're having tea, or before we play, while we're practicing. While improvising, I give my full attention to the music, to flow, and I save the work of critical analysis for later.

Flow is the intuitive and embodied reality of the music itself. If long tones are part of my flow, I play long tones. If the bass player plays an ostinato, I work with that, not because it's "good," but because it *is*. If the piano player begins a solo with an unexpected dissonance, I don't judge or question their choice, I embrace the dissonance because they played it. It's never a question of good or bad, right or wrong, like or dislike. When I'm fully immersed in the music, judgment is irrelevant.

To disrupt judgmental thinking, avoid asking yourself these deadly questions:

1) Do I like this?
2) Is this good?
3) What kind of music is this?
4) Why is this happening?

Art: First of all, it isn't bad if these thoughts come up, but imagine if you were meeting a person for the first time, just as you're meeting this piece for the first time. You don't want your old prejudices to block your ability to sense. So, when these questions come up, just put them in a drawer.

The first question is, "Do I like it or not?" Look, you don't know anything! Even if you decide that you like this music, this is a barrier because you're thinking, "Well, now I've decided that I like it, so I don't have to listen anymore. I can tell somebody else that I liked it, or I can tell somebody else that I didn't like it. I'm safe now."

The second question is, "Is this good?" Is this legitimate, excellent, or worthy? Is this a good film? Is this a worthy human being? Again, what do you know about that, really? Judgments can happen in the first instant, but these are just your prejudices and your fears, so put them in a drawer. Be open to learning about the piece or the person. A first impression may be misleading—for sure it isn't the whole story.

The third one is, "What kind of music is this?" Is it the kind I like? Is it the kind I know about? Is it jazz? Is it reggae? Well, you don't know what's going to happen, so just listen.

Mark: I think another deadly question is, "Why?" Why is the bass player playing that note? Why did the drummer stop playing? We don't have to understand someone else's motivation, we just work with what's going on.

Art: Your understanding of what's happening may be very different from someone else in the band, or the audience, or yourself in the next moment. Your judgment isn't the truth. It's a shortcut to say, "I know this piece; it should go like this...." Well, just when you think the piece is loud and raucous, it could shift to gentle and spacious for the next section, or maybe we'll discover an element that we didn't notice before.

What I ask instead is, "What do you sense?" We try to get at our actual experience, rather than our prejudices, habits, or judgments. Then we get personal insights: "It was very calm at the beginning and then it got more active. Those sounds scared me, or they reminded me of my summers in Maine. I noticed that there were a lot of high sounds." Good! You were actually there, and it wasn't about whether you liked it or not, or whether it was good or not, or what kind of music it was, because maybe that doesn't matter so much.

Mark: Judgment separates us from the music. Judgement takes us out of flow.

Art: And it takes you out of curiosity, which is what really carries the energy of presence. Just being interested in it, in itself, and not thinking that you're making it happen, but just, here's the sound. Now what? What does it feel like? How does it move? All the things that bring you into the actual experience rather than codify it or justify it.

Mark: And judgment is rooted in ego: Am I an excellent musician? Is my playing legitimate? Is this music good? Am I good?

Art: And ego is usually a lack of so-called confidence; but in full confidence, this doesn't even come up.

The devil card in the tarot deck I created is called "Vanity."[1]Rather than the problems in life coming from outside of you—whether it's that the acoustics are bad in the room, or you didn't practice enough, or the critic didn't like it, or the band didn't rehearse enough, or you don't know the piece, or the world is unfair and judges you—vanity is all between you and you. The picture is of a mirror, like in Snow White, a blank mirror. If you look in the mirror, you're either going to say it's great or it's not great. So, don't look in the mirror.

Raccoons don't look in the mirror to see if they run well or eat in an interesting way. They don't know what that looks like. They don't have a self-concept. On the tarot card, there's the mirror and wallpaper with clapping hands. The instruction about vanity is if you look in the mirror, you're looking at what you do rather than just doing what you do or being how you are. When you look in the mirror, you're trying to see what it is, and whether it's good or not.

Clapping hands or no clapping hands, it's the same problem. Am I great or am I bad? No, I'm just here. There's no devil outside who's tempting you. It's you who are tempted to look in the mirror and judge good or bad. And then you imagine that everybody else is looking at you when they're not. Nobody cares what you do. As you're playing your first phrase, nobody is noticing whether it's great or not, they're just listening.

Vanity is another word for ego. Ego can't resist objectifying self. If you leave the mirror out, then you can just do your thing like any plant or

---

[1] Art designed his own tarot deck, *The Art Tarot*. For more information go to artlande.com.

animal that doesn't have a sense of, "I'm a big tree" or "I'm a small tree,"
or "I have a disease." They're just being, I think [laughs]. I don't really
know.

Flow is the Underlying Stillness

Flow isn't the notes we play. Flow is the underlying stillness, the source
of the music. We have to be careful to relate to source, and not fall in
love with the activity of note making. It might feel good to play lots of
notes and rhythms, but in doing so, you might be out of synch with the
rest of the music, out of touch with the generative quality of stillness
and flow. The question is, are you playing your notes in relation to
source? Are you listening?

Art: When you say the word "flow," people think of air flow or water-
flow that doesn't start and stop. But flow in this sense isn't incessant. Flow
includes breath and silence. In flow, we can pause or end. If you're getting
your flow only through what you're doing, you risk getting attached to
certain ways of playing because they're agreeable, and the body gets
acclimated. I'm not saying that the body isn't a part of music, because it
is, but if you must go to that to be comfortable, you're not sensing flow
through silence.

Flow can include change. The music can go faster or slower; it can be
loud or soft, active or still. That's flow for me. The through line is the
silence, like the way our friend Jerry Granelli plays with his sticks in the
air and nothing is hitting the drum set, and then you hear, "Ba Da!" and
it's so right, and it's alive in the beat because it's part of flow.

Allowing it in

Art: Jerry Granelli helped me understand that music comes out of this
moving silence. Right now, this is what I need to play, or this is what is
sounding, and my job is to render that. It has to happen, like springtime
coming out of this snow. When is it time for the flower or the tree to bud?
The tree is not thinking, "Well, when would it be cool?" It just happens.
There's an inevitability in it. This has to get played now, in this way.

Mark: So, we can trust the silence. We can trust the nothing because it's moving somewhere.

Art: Yes, and it's inviting either more of itself, or something needs to happen. But it doesn't say, "Come on! When are you going to play something?" I think about the rests in classical music. If the musicians are really into it, they're "playing" the rests; they're playing 78 bars of nothing and then when they enter, the music emerges out of something organic. But if the nothing is not a living thing, if they're lazy and just reading the newspaper, when they enter it isn't the same. And people can tell. People feel it when you lurch, when what you play is not connected to the silence that precedes it. When it's disconnected, it's inappropriate or too loud or too something. It doesn't ring true, and it doesn't feel good.

Chapter 5

Roles and Relationships

Sensation and imagination, openness and flow, sharing your story in fidelity with whatever happens in the moment—this is the inner path of the improviser. But what about the rest of the band? In a quintet there are five points of view, five sources of personal inspiration, five variations on present moment awareness. How do we work with all that difference? How do we form a musical community that celebrates the experience of each individual while creating a sensible and satisfying whole?

Improvisation allows us to tell our stories through our relationships. The success of the music depends on the quality of our interactions in community with one another. The contemporary jazz trumpet player Wynton Marsalis calls this a "negotiation," (Burns, 2001b) but that term implies willful struggle and, in the end, winners and losers. In true collaboration, there is no struggle; there is only the mutual embrace of possibility. Whatever one person plays catalyzes the others in response and vice versa. Ultimately, our allegiance is not to an individual creative vision—mine or yours—but to the creative output of the ensemble as a whole. We influence one another. We share the responsibilities of leadership, but no one is consistently in control. Working together, we willingly serve the greater good of the music itself.

Art: I don't have to fight to prove that my sense of reality is the most important; I think we need all points of view. If you are humble enough to invite in other sensibilities, including the history of the music, and people who are into quarter tones, and others who are interested in noise or the resonance of the overtone series, all of these things become relevant. All of these perspectives are viable and important.

This is the additive principle. We simply add my idea to yours rather than choose one or the other. If I add an elephant to your picture of a cabin, we have a cabin/elephant picture, assuming I don't use the elephant to block the cabin. I'm trying to get drummers to understand this. Can you offer a beat without saying "This is the beat!" in a way that makes it impossible for us not to be interested in it? Here's an elephant and a cabin, but you've made the elephant so big that the cabin is gone. That's not elephant and cabin anymore. That's "Well, I want to do elephant and the cabin doesn't matter."

I don't like thinking that if I play this, *then you should play* that. *Why would you go there? If you need me to make a tree instead of an elephant because you think the tree goes better with your cabin, we have a problem as improvisers. Either compose a tree part for me or use your creativity and flexibility to accept and integrate the cabin plus elephant. Don't try to think for me or control me; just play your own part.*

We need to work on ways of sensing what's available to us and making all of it inclusive and additive. You think we can't have that person in the band because they play out of tune? Well, we can have some out-of-tuneness in the band. Why can't that be part of our universe if we really like the energy of that person, or that person feels like they belong. Why can't we expand into that?

I feel that whatever is played needs to be there. If somebody plays some corny beat or cliché, then it's included when it occurs naturally.

Musical Relationships

Collaboration is not about compromise—giving in or giving something up—as much as it is a willingness to remain flexible in support of the collective good. On an interpersonal level, successful collaboration celebrates both individual integrity and musical connection. In effect, the ensemble and I become a single, multicellular whole. Difference is not a problem. Our differences inspire and enliven us, and serve as a spur to further creative activity.

One key to successful collaboration is understanding the nature of musical relationships, recognizing what they are and how they shift over time. Here are six of the most basic relationships or roles we can play in an ensemble:

1) Mimic
2) Soloist
3) Accompanist
4) Co-soloist
5) Destroyer
6) Relationship of no relationship

Mimic (Matching)
Perhaps the simplest relationship we can have with another person is to mirror what that person is doing or saying. Children learn to talk by mimicking the sounds of their parents' voices. They learn about the world through careful observation and by copying what they hear and see.

One way to enter an improvisation is to match what someone else is playing, to merge with that person, to embody what you hear by playing it as you hear it. This can serve to reinforce or clarify a part that might otherwise be overlooked.

Soloist (The Speaker)
The soloist is our speaker or narrator. They tell us how it feels to be in the environment created by the rest of the band. If the band creates a place, like a meadow, the soloist dances in that meadow. The soloist asserts their creative vision, thereby establishing a focus and musical direction for the ensemble.

Accompanist (Complement or Contrast)

The accompanist provides a foundation for the soloist, helping them uncover and develop their creative ideas. The accompanist supports the soloist by adding a layer that enriches the musical environment. If the soloist creates a full moon, the accompanist can add a tree or some stars, or a lonely person in the distance.

An accompanying part is usually simpler, quieter, less active, and more repetitive than the solo. Examples of traditional accompanying parts are bass lines, chords, an ostinato (repeating pattern), or long tones that outline the harmony. The accompanying part doesn't have to match what the soloist is doing. The accompanist can also create contrast; they can add spice or dissonance as long as they're careful not to overwhelm the solo. The accompanist adds a supportive element that either complements or contrasts with what the soloist plays.

Non-traditional accompanying parts can include any sound that provides an interesting timbre or texture in the background, including electronic sounds, non-traditional instrumental sounds (squeaks, squawks, breathing, scraping, tapping, plucking) environmental and found sounds such as rain, crickets, crumpling paper, the sound of a rickety wooden chair, or traffic noise. One of my favorite sounds is the rusty hinge of an old car ashtray that I keep in my instrument bag; its little shrieks are like the cries of a dystopian insect. It would be impossible to solo on this "instrument," but it can contribute an interesting texture to the environment. In short, the accompanist provides the background, while the soloist provides the foreground. The accompanist is the place; the soloist is the thing in the place.

Art: As a pianist, I create harmonies where the soloist will succeed no matter what they play and not be thrown into right and wrong about notes. I don't play too often. I mix two white keys, two black keys, or one white and one black willy-nilly, higher and lower, with no system or sense. People often tell me that everything they do works, which is the highest compliment for an accompanist.

Co-Soloist (Adding a New Element)
An alternative to the traditional soloist/accompanist relationship is the dual role of the co-soloist. Any two (or more) musicians can "solo" at the same time, sharing the musical spotlight. The interaction between or among co-soloists can range from an energetic shouting match to carefully interwoven melodic lines and interactive call and response. Like the accompanist, the co-soloist adds an element that either complements or contrasts with what the other soloist is doing, but both parts are equally prominent.

In the first example, the co-soloists match each other's energies like two drunks in a bar. If one soloist creates a high level of intensity, the other matches that intensity, but neither is too concerned about refined communication.

Alternatively, co-soloists can create an orderly dialog, each listening carefully to the other while interweaving complementary melodic lines. This contrapuntal relationship is respectful and responsive. Neither part is subordinate to the other. Two lovers read Rumi in the moonlight.

A co-soloist duet might also follow the traditional call and response format. One partner offers a phrase, and the other listens and replies. This interchange is sometimes described as "question and answer," a conversation where the first phrase functions as a question with the second as its answer.

Destroyer (Going Against, Causing a Problem, Playing Defense)
A fifth possible role is that of the destroyer or, if you prefer a less aggressive term, the recycler, or channel changer. After an improvisation has run its course, the best choice might be to start a revolution, to destroy what is no longer needed by initiating something new.

"Destruction," in this sense, is a creative choice, not an act of aggression. When the creative potential of an improvisation is exhausted (or almost exhausted), the destroyer determines that the time has come for fundamental change. The destroyer then offers a new musical idea so radical that the new cannot be seen as a further development of the old. The destroyer causes an utterly different music to emerge. Everything changes as the old music ends and something new begins.

Art: I call it going against, causing a problem or playing defense. People say, "There's no defense in music!" Well, there is if I'm playing. See if you can play your thing while I play a little slower than you in the wrong key....

One time with the Rubisa Patrol I was playing a solo ballad—really beautiful—and then about three quarters of the way through, the rest of the Rubisas got up and started playing this funk thing, right in front of the audience, really loud, and they held up a sign while they were doing it. I didn't blink, I just played to the end of my solo. The people were laughing; it was so cool. I just did what I was doing, and when it ended. I asked them about the sign. It said, "Fuck Art, Let's Dance." It wasn't about me, you know. I thought that was great, and they planned it unbeknownst to me, and they did it during my beautiful, precious ballad. I loved it, of course. That's serious defense.

Silly antics, theater, and poetry can be used to keep things from becoming overly predictable. Humor, surrealism, and sudden shifts in mood are tools we can use to keep the audience and the band on their toes. The complacency and security of thinking that you know what's happening or what's going to happen next is broken, as it is in real life. A squirrel runs onto the field during the eighth inning of a tense World Series game, causing a gleeful chase. A friend has a seizure at dinner or goes into a deep depression that lasts for a month. I prefer music to be like life rather than an idealized, perfect, better-than-life experience. But too much theater or too many antics can be indulgent rather than surprising. They can become deadening, unrealistic, and no fun, so these things have to be mixed in judiciously, whether they are planned or happen spontaneously.

Subtle Disruption

If the music gets a little stale or self-satisfied, you can add an element that confounds or delights the ear but isn't meant to overthrow the social order. Things that are clearly absurd, silly, weird, or annoying are added to the prevailing story: stride piano or rock n' roll in the middle of a serious twelve-tone piece, playing slightly slower or faster than the prevailing tempo, or offering a few banal chords or rhythms can help aerate the music by subtly disturbing the status quo. The intention here is not to create a reaction in the other players or cause them to change what they're doing; the effect might be humor, puzzlement, disorientation, freshness, or amazement as the music continues. In the middle of a 17th century English drama, some L.A. hipsters drive up to the manor in a convertible playing rap music on the radio while talking about designer drugs. Or two couples are eating dinner at a fancy restaurant; a walrus in a bad toupee pulls up a chair at the table next to them and sits quietly reading Chaucer.

Art: I like doing things that integrate but are somehow insidious, like putting something in the room that really doesn't fit but also doesn't ask for attention. It's played as if it's almost not be noticed because you don't project it at all. To accomplish this, I think it's important to notice what your intention is. I can play something to try to wreck everything, but I can also do it just to see if anyone notices.

The successful destroyer (or subtle disruptor) knows that timing is everything. A sudden change in musical direction is an effective choice when the piece is stuck or the musicians have grown complacent. The destroyer/disruptor clears away the old by offering something new and unexpected. But, a word of caution. Sudden change can be welcome, like a plunge into icy water in the middle of summer, but unexpected change can also be damaging. If destruction is imposed at an inopportune time or if a developing piece hasn't completely run its course, premature destruction can engender feelings of disappointment and a sense of wasted opportunity in the other musicians.

Ahimsa is a Sanskrit word that describes an important creative principle: Do no harm. In improvising together, this principle is fundamental to developing trust within the ensemble. If you wield the sword of creative destruction, do so only in the spirit of ahimsa, not self-aggrandizement or bullying. The purpose of creative destruction is to recycle used-up materials so that something fresh can take their place.

In the aftermath of destruction, everyone in the ensemble is confronted with a choice. Imagine a long, lyrical meditation on sound and stillness. Now imagine that during this introspective exploration the bass player realizes (just ahead of everyone else) that the music is starting to sound a little precious, maybe even boring, so they initiate a blues shuffle while singing loudly about their recent trip to Las Vegas and all the money they won playing blackjack. The drummer jumps in and their timing is perfect: The audience laughs, the musicians are startled, but they're smiling. This is effective destruction, a true channel change.

At this point, the other musicians need to make a decision. Do they drop what they're doing and follow the bass player and drummer to Las Vegas? Or do they continue on their quiet way, creating a weird juxtaposition of old and new? They may feel that the new direction is so compelling that they have to submit to it, or they might present the old and new together like a split-screen image in film, which might lead to an exploration of paradox, difference, irony, absurdity, or comedy. Either choice will lead the improvisation in an intriguing new direction.

Trust

I've performed and recorded with Art since the early 1970s. We've played music together thousands of times in hundreds of different venues. Art is fearless, versatile, and highly skilled—one of the best, a world-class improviser. Early in our relationship, I was soloing and he was accompanying me on a beautiful ballad. As I was losing myself in my creative reverie, Art stopped playing. He suddenly abandoned the relationship of soloist and accompanist, and I didn't know why. I found myself in free fall, as if the stage had disappeared under my feet.

As we talked about it later, I realized that he had made an interesting creative choice. He sensed that our duet would benefit from the intimacy and immediacy of the saxophone alone; he wanted to hear the solo saxophone, not just a saxophone solo. I wasn't prepared to trust such a seemingly radical decision at the time, but now, after many years of working together, I trust Art's musical sensibilities completely. Now I would carry on without question.

Art's sense of musical possibility is practically boundless. He often offers creative ideas that are unexpected and sometimes even a little disconcerting. He can create a sense of groundless possibility that some musicians find liberating and others find irritating—or worse. But whether I feel grounded or groundless is irrelevant. I know that I have nothing to fear. Trust is an essential part of the path.

Exercise: Discovering Your Role

Step 1.
Musician #1: begins to play a short, simple motif (a simple musical idea), repeating it as accurately as possible, cycling it over and over.
Musician #2: As the motif is repeated, Musician #2 begins to mimic (copy) the motif as precisely as they can, until both are cycling the motif seamlessly together. If Musician #2 can't duplicate the motif exactly (especially if the musicians are playing two very different instruments, like drums and piano), they should copy the notes and rhythms of the motif as best they can.

Step 2.
Musician #1: continues to repeat the motif.
Musician #2: begins to solo, treating the original motif as a background or accompanying part.

Step 3.
Musician #2: returns to the original motif.

<u>Musician #1:</u> begins to solo, treating the motif as a background or accompanying part.

Step 4.
Both musicians begin to solo together, neither one overshadowing the other. This co-solo can take any of the forms described above (call and response, interweaving, etc.)

Step 5.
One of the musicians wrecks the settled aesthetic by playing something so radically different from what's gone before that it that destroys any possibility of continuing.

Take your time. Stay with each step until the relationships are clearly established.

The Relationship of No Relationship (Existing Together)

According to Chögyam Trungpa (2005), "The arrival of chaos should be regarded as extremely good news" (p. 26). When musical events appear to have no clear relationship, when things happen at random or by accident, our job is not to "fix" the music, our job is to welcome what is. Someone is painting my kitchen; I come home, make a sandwich, and eat it. Events don't have to be relational; they can simply exist together. If I don't understand what's going on, that isn't a problem. I mind my own business. I play whatever I want to play or just listen without shutting down or tuning out. Chaos is good news when we trust each other, and when we trust the creative viability of whatever happens.

Art: The audience gets to put it together however they want. They create the relationship because the relationship isn't literal; there's not an obvious link.

Exercise: Minding Your Own Business

Step 1. Two musicians play together without discussing the music beforehand. Each plays something specific, but no agreement is made about the key, chord progression, meter, style, or any other musical parameter. Neither knows what the other is about to do.

On cue, both begin their separate parts. The musicians simply listen as the music unfolds. Neither player adapts to the other, neither makes any adjustment whatsoever. Listeners are invited to stay present with the delight or discomfort of their experience.

Step 2. Repeat the process, choosing something new to play. As the two musicians listen to the randomly created music, each begins to consider how they might adapt their part to clarify their relationship. If one person's part is more complex than the other, they may continue their relationship as soloist and accompanist. If both parts seem equally energetic, they may continue as co-soloists. If their relationship is ambiguous, the two must decide individually how they would like the piece to proceed and make adjustments to their playing in order to establish a clear relationship. Afterwards, discuss the exercise with the listeners. Were the relationships clearly established? Why or why not?

The Four Karmas

Another way to establish a clear relationship with the music and the other musicians is to consider the principle of cause and effect. According to the Tibetan Buddhist tradition, we can contribute to any situation by offering our energies in one of the following ways, called the "four karmas."

1) Pacifying energy. When the music is turbulent or fractured, adding more mojo to the mix might not be that helpful. You could instead play something pacifying or calming, refocusing a piece that threatens to fly apart.

2) Enriching energy. If the piece is developing well, you can strengthen or enrich the music as it plays. You don't have to

add anything especially innovative or creative, simply join the party.

3) Magnetizing energy. From a compositional perspective, music needs to move forward, to develop, in order to thrive. If the piece becomes too static or repetitious, an energetic quantum leap might be necessary. You can magnetize or draw fresh energy into the piece by offering an inspiring new idea or creative direction. When things get stuck, you can give the music a push.

4) Destruction. As above, creative destruction may be appropriate when the piece has run its course and we need to clear a path for whatever happens next. In destruction, the old is composted for the sake of new growth.

What Role Should I Take? The Prime Directive

We can find our role by noticing and then playing whatever the piece needs. Anyone can fill any role at any time. If the music lacks rhythmic energy or precision, I can play something rhythmic. If melody hasn't been heard for a while, anyone on any instrument can offer a melody. If a bass line would help solidify the piece, play that. If the entire enterprise lacks focus, someone can lead the way by soloing.

Roles and relationships should be fluid, not habitual. If your preference is to remain in the background, challenge yourself to step forward and tell your story. If your first impulse is to copy or mimic what someone else is doing, remember that there are other ways to serve the music. If your habit is always to be the first to solo, you can contribute by leaving space for others to tell their story. Be willing to respond to the needs of the group and the music as a whole. This is the Prime Directive: serve the music.

Chapter 6

Spontaneous Composition

The way Louis Armstrong played was "more free" than earlier players. Roy Eldridge was "more free" than his predecessors. Dizzy Gillespie was another stage and [Don] Cherry was another. And you have to keep it going otherwise you lose that freedom. And then the music is finished. It's a matter of life and death. The only criterion is: "Is this stuff alive or is it dead?"
—Steve Lacy (as cited in Bailey, 1993, p. 56)

Oh yeah? Free from what?
—Jerry Granelli (n.d.)

Just as composers develop their ideas with clarity and economy of means, our goal is to improvise with precision and formal integrity. The freedom that Steve Lacy mentions above—and it *is* a matter of life and death—is the freedom to be yourself and follow the source of your own music. We are free to tell our story, but at the same time, we are bound by our commitment to community. We are also bound by the requirements of craft and musicianship.

In improvisation, we work with the same musical elements found in formal composition. A partial list of these elements might include:

- dissonance/consonance
- complexity/simplicity
- intensity/calm
- density/spaciousness
- range (high and low)
- dynamics (loud and soft)
- texture/timbre
- melody

- phrasing (breathing)
- articulation
- harmony
- form
- repetition
- imitation
- sequence
- development
- recapitulation
- bass lines
- rhythm (motion)
- groove
- pulse
- tempo
- feel
- technique
- intonation
- juxtaposition
- humor/seriousness
- urgency/relaxation
- light/dark
- precise/diffuse
- tradition/non-tradition
- compliance/resistance
- surprise
- etc.

All of this happens spontaneously, while we're playing. We can't stop to think about what we're doing; we can't edit or take time out to plan what happens next.

Art: The students often say, "Well, this all sounds nice, but how do we do it?" They want to Google it and then have the answer, but this is not the computer world. You have to live it out. It's challenging to trust the process, and also to let the process reveal something different than what you thought it would.

We begin with stillness. Our task is be open, curious and ready to play. We listen, and then play what we want to hear, as well as we can.

The Most Powerful Thing You Ever Heard at a Jazz Club

Art: I remember playing at Dazzle, a Denver jazz club, with the Cuddle Band. In that band, we invite you to lie down for the concert. Instead of a dance floor, we have a cuddle area. We want you to feel relaxed as we wait for the music to show up, and we're not going to play until it arrives. You can rest as we wait for the music to come over the hill. This is at a major jazz club, right? One of the first times we played there, there was nothing for minutes on end, and of course, that's the most powerful thing you ever heard at a jazz club. Then Amy Shelley, our drummer, just went, Pow! And it was so good. It didn't feel forced at all. Out of this crescendo of nothing comes her big drum hit. We are getting comfortable with perception, with just being, instead of "I have to do something right now and I have to do something great."

Open possibility gives way to something specific as the first notes sound. The music crystalizes and the piece develops an identity—*these* tones, *these* chords, *this* rhythm, a certain dynamic level, and a particular feel. Just as classical musicians read the score of a composition, improvisers "read" the sounds that emerge from stillness. As we listen, we begin the work of spontaneous composition.

The key is to notice the qualities of the music as it begins to emerge. Is the dynamic level loud or soft? Is the texture sparse or dense? Is there a soloist? Is there a pulse, bass line, or rhythmic groove? What is the emotional feel or mood of the piece? Which instruments are involved? Are the sounds consonant or dissonant, unified or fragmented? We identify the musical elements in play and work with them to develop our improvisation over time. Spontaneous composition begins when we commit to a particular musical focus, a specific point of view.

In the beginning, we accept whatever arises. We don't need validation or confirmation, either internally or externally. If you follow your sense of curiosity and are willing to work with whatever comes to you in the moment, the fact that it arises is validation enough.

Art: People feel that the present moment is inadequate because they won't give themselves to it, including "I'm tired" or "I'm bored" or "This whole thing is making me nervous." And I think there are issues about acknowledgment. On my phone I get smiley faces and lots of "likes," but it's ambiguous when you're playing. Did the listeners like it? Do I like it? Do you like it? Do you think I'm great? Do you think I'm worthy? Am I better than I was yesterday?

Mark: We learn to look for approval rather than experience the deep satisfaction of working with whatever happens in the moment.

Art: It's about disconnection from the body. If I play something and I feel beauty or interest in it, I'm not worried about whether anyone in the audience or in the band feels the same. It's just fine for me to play those three tones and find them satisfying in my body or in my ear, and they open something for me. But I think people have so much insecurity that when they feel inclined to play the thing they hear, they discount their idea because they assume it's not good enough.

Development

We assume that any idea that arises out of conscious listening is "good enough." The simplest musical idea, a *motif*, is a seed that can grow into a satisfying composition or improvisation when we work to unlock its creative potential. The obvious example is Beethoven's Symphony #5. Beethoven developed his iconic four note opening over the course of an entire symphonic movement, exploring the many creative possibilities suggested by his one simple motif. Similarly, the opening phrase of Duke Ellington's "Africa Flower" contains just two alternating tones that unfold into a jazz classic.

Development happens when a musical element—a melody, chord progression, rhythm, texture, dynamic, or other musical parameter— is shaped and reshaped over time. A melody can be expanded or contracted, a rhythm can be varied rather than discarded, a part can be played in different styles or modes. The possibilities are almost endless.

Exercise: Developing a Musical Motif

Compose a simple melody of three to five notes. Anything will do, the simpler the better. Write your melody on a piece of staff paper or commit it to memory.

Just as in composition, in improvisation it's usually more effective to explore the potential of one or two succinct ideas than to string together a bunch of unrelated thoughts, stream of consciousness style.

You don't have to come up with a ton of ideas, you can choose one or two and rework them in different ways. Here are twenty-six possible permutations you can try with a single motif.

1. Repeat the motif as is
2. Omit notes
3. Add a note from above or below a given note
4. Add notes from above and below (encircle) a given note
5. Strike the original note, add notes, then return to the original note
6. Repeat notes that are not repeated, or "un-repeat" notes that are repeated in the motif
7. Octave displacement: instead of going up to a note, go down to the same note one octave lower. Instead of repeating a note, go up or down an octave to the same note.
8. Connect notes with intervallic sequences or rhythmic patterns
9. Condense/expand: remove or add space to the motif
10. Tempo: play it faster or slower
11. Vary the rhythm
12. Add another phrase to the motif
13. Spokes of a wheel: use a long tone as a pedal point to reach out from and return to before proceeding
14. Fragmentation: use only part of the motif
15. Scramble the notes of the motif
16. Turn the motif upside down
17. Retrograde: play the motif backwards
18. Modulation: change key
19. Change mode: for example, if the motif is set in a major scale, play it in a minor scale
20. Vary the harmonic setting: choose different chords to accompany the motif
21. Vary the style: e.g., play it in a classical style, then play it with a reggae feel

22. Vary the dynamics: e.g., play it loud or soft, or start loud and get softer as you go
23. Keep the rhythm and change the notes
24. Pitch bend: slide up or down to a note, or strike the note and then bend it up or down
25. Vary the timbre: change the sound quality of the note; instead of rich and full, play or sing it rough and breathy
26. Combinations of the above

Phrasing and Melodic Line

Melody is the singable part of music, the pleasing series of tones that captures our attention at the center of a folk song, pop hit, or jazz standard like "Someday My Prince Will Come," or "Yesterday" by the Beatles. In creating a melody, we sometimes work with a motif, as in John Coltrane's "A Love Supreme," or a melodic line can unwind like a string of beads ("Wave" by Antonio Carlos Jobim). A melody can also sound jagged, with emphatic leaps and sharp edges ("Freedom Jazz Dance" by Eddie Harris.)

According to the composer Igor Stravinsky, there can be no effective theory of melody making. Melody is a gift of the imagination guided by intuition. In creating a melodic line, the goal is to satisfy the ear. A melody can be drawn from a scale or key, the tones can be connected chromatically using notes from outside the scale or key, or it can sound atonal, using notes that have no discernible relationship to scale or key. But don't overthink it; if it sounds right, it is right.

As we improvise a melody, we often shape the tones into phrases that have a beginning, middle, and end, just like the phrases and sentences in conversational speech. A melodic phrase asks a question or makes a clear statement. In between phrases, we pause and breathe. Without phrasing, note making can sound haphazard or arbitrary, communicating nothing in particular to the listener.

Art: When I work with singers, instead of having them sing their song, "All of Me" or whatever it is, I ask them to sing the text of a poem. They take the phrasing from the words of the poem, but they can make up the notes. This can apply to any instrument. When I notice that a person's phrasing is not alive, I ask them to play what's in the poetry book. They make shapes of melody using phrases, rhythms, and accents from the poem.

Thinking Like a Composer

Content is what we play—the notes, rhythms, and phrases that we bring to life on our instruments. Form is how content is structured and developed over time, revealing a coherent musical storyline. In composed music, form helps to articulate a complex musical journey that can include multiple sections and highly refined developmental processes. In improvisation, form evolves organically as we shape the music over the course of an entire piece. An improvisation can include different sections, repetition, transitions, and developmental change.

Without form, an improvisation becomes (at best) a colorful sound collage or (at worst) an incoherent mess of individual ideas with no clear relationship or collective purpose. Whether composed or improvised, form can provide inspiration, clarity, and a pathway forward for the musicians. As improvisers, we need to pay attention to both content and form, to the creative process of music making in the moment, and to the developmental arc of music making over time.

Art: I definitely function more as a composer than as a player, even when I'm improvising completely fresh material. I'm thinking the same as I would as I compose—that what we need here is a slow part, or that this part is for the bass and the drums only. Here I solo. It's just that it hasn't been decided beforehand. I realize the composition in the moment, and it can be quite clear about mood and different sections and thematic material. It's not random—a little of this and a little of that. It's not a Whitman's sampler.

I was talking to somebody about an indulgent band that they're in where they're not thinking about composition. Instead, they're thinking, "I'm having fun playing, so I'm going to keep going rather than end this section even though it's wearing out, or that it needs to expand, develop or transform." They're thinking, "I like doing this over and over again, even though it's driving everyone crazy," or "I like soloing really long and loud because it's fun for me," or "I'm only going to solo short because I'm not in the mood," rather than creating what the piece really needs.

We can offer contrast when there's too much sameness—e.g., play low tones because we haven't heard any for a while. We can join in a rhythm and let it prevail, and let it go when it's used up. We need to recognize what's happening and hear forward, hear what happens next. Therefore, you need to label the area you're working in, not just the thing you're playing in the moment. For instance, to notice that we're being contrapuntal (playing two or more melodies at the same time.) Instead of that lasting for only a moment, we can work with "contrapuntality" in general. Maybe you and I start and then we add a third voice, or somebody replaces you. We can have a whole contrapuntal section instead of just a single event. But you have to give it a chapter heading so you can see it beyond just that moment, to generalize from the specific and let it develop in various ways.

Orchestration, ideation, harmonization, or dynamics—you can use an idea until it comes to some kind of fruition. We can work with pitch, creating interest by playing weird intervals or notes that don't normally belong with the harmony. We can work with quarter tones or bent notes—anything that will support a whole section, or a whole piece. We can drop the form in composed music or create form in open music. We can add chords or rhythm when those elements have been absent.

The great French guitarist Nguyên Lê works with sound worlds, sonorities that have a discernible character. If you find a distinct sound environment, whether it's your own sound or a band sound—drummers playing only on a tom, the saxophone playing low without any attack, bells and gongs, toy instruments, or electronics—anything that establishes a palpable soundscape or environment can sustain a whole section of a piece. Again, we should be selective. If everybody is playing the same instruments the same way all of the time, the sound world isn't intriguing for the listener.

Hear it Forward

Art: You have to be able to sense how things proceed when there's no script. This is challenging for people who are used to being told what to do, or who do things out of habit instead of sensing what they would like to hear and what would feel good to all of us. Can I really create the next thing without the composer or the conductor or my guru telling me? Can I really hear into what continues?

Mark: So, there's the skill of hearing what's happening right now and exploring its creative potential. And then there's an act of the imagination, being able to hear forward to what happens next. Sometimes people don't hear the potential of what's going on. They might not notice the contrapuntal event, so they wouldn't know to label it and then develop it. Or they don't notice when another musician plays something that might signify the beginning of a solo or a new section. If nobody notices, the piece can't go anywhere.

Art: We need to recognize what happens and give it language, and then take responsibility for staying with it or playing whatever opens up the next thing. At the same time, we can't become distracted by worrying about what happens next; we need to trust that it will work itself out. If we remember a section of a piece, we can return to it later, maybe in a shortened version or at a different speed. This is common in classical music, of course. We can create forms like ABCAD (where each letter represents a different section of the piece), realizing that we may want to return to some earlier material (section A) by naming it, remembering it, playing it, and then making a transition to a new section to end the piece (section D).

Also, this is communal; the whole world is there too. The sun is helping me decide what I want to do next. The audience is helping with their energy. The band is helping. If I don't know how to proceed, well, maybe the other musicians know perfectly well and I don't have to do anything.

You Can Stop

Art: We were teaching at Cornish College of the Arts, you, me, and Julian Priester.[1] The students had never improvised without a preconceived plan or a song, and I suggested that each of us say one thing to them, just one thing that might help them on their way.

So, you said your forgettable thing, and I said my forgettable thing, and then Julian, in his inimitable manner: "Julian, what do you have to tell them?" He was their teacher, you know, the guy who they were working

---

[1] Julian Priester is a trombonist and former member of the Duke Ellington Orchestra, Herbie Hancock's Headhunters, and many other influential bands.

with regularly. He said nothing for about two minutes, which is his way, and everybody's trying to sense what might matter to him, and he says, "You can stop." Everyone laughed and I said, "You have the right teacher."

Due to our speedy world and our active minds, people don't know how to end anything. They don't know how to come out of their addiction to "It's fun to do this," or "I'm sick of doing it, but I'm ashamed that it wasn't good, so I'm going to keep going." Some people have a hard time ending a piece or ending their solo. It's hard for them to come out of the music and just listen or make a different environment.

We had a duo class at the University of Colorado recently, and maybe this is even more difficult in a duo. In a piano/trumpet duet, the trumpet player would stop, the piano player would emerge and there'd be a different texture; we would hear just the piano. But then the trumpet player would immediately start playing again. It was hard for them to be silent.

When the other person is playing, that's also you; you're just speaking through them, through a different medium. Because you're in this piece together you can just listen, but that's you playing. I call it waiting in the weeds. Wait for the moment when you're needed to continue the story or add to the texture. Don't go out and then come right back in, disappear for a while. Let the others tell the story for you.

So, Julian said, "You can stop." I love that. The students remembered it. They played something for a while, and then it would end. I don't remember anything about what you and I said at all [laughs].

How do you know when to stop? How do you know when the piece is over, or when to bring your solo to a close? The composer Pierre Boulez famously dismissed improvisation as "personal psychodrama," (as cited in Lewis, n.d.), as if improvised music were nothing more than cathartic release. If that were the case, you would know that your solo was over when you ran out of gas. This is not our view.

The answer to the question "When should I stop?" is found within the larger context of the piece. Each improvisation and each element within it, including solos and accompanying parts, develops along a natural arc. We can think of the arc of an improvised piece or solo as an inquiry into a specific topic or question that we want to investigate—a melody or rhythm, a texture or sound environment, a sonority or dissonance.

Art: A student asked me about this at CalArts. "How do I know when my solo is over?" I told them that each solo has three parts: a point of inquiry, development, and realization. I don't end until I've realized something about our inquiry. The solo is over when we've discovered something.

The inquiry is developed with the whole band. The soloist says, "Let's look in these caves!" And then you find a cave painting or a rock or you find a way out. "What happens if we keep getting softer and softer?" or "What's up with these short atonal notes?" We investigate, and we realize something through our inquiry.

Mark: You've also made the point that you have to stay with the inquiry long enough for people to understand what it is that you're exploring.

Art: Exactly right. It takes time for the band to make some headway. I need to complete the inquiry in my solo; or if somebody else is soloing, I want them to do that. We're all working together toward that end. The audience is also trying to understand and relate to it, to know what it is, to feel that the inquiry is developing and will have some sense of satisfaction and completion.

Different developmental arcs occur simultaneously in an improvisation. At the most elemental level, as I play my instrument I am aware of the development of a single tone from its beginning, or attack, to the middle, which may include changes in volume and variations in timbre and pitch, to its end or release, which may be sudden or gradual. On an even more minute level, I am aware of my breath and, supporting that, my posture, all of which affects my ability to control the attack, shape, and release of a single tone.

Beyond that one note, I am aware of the development of my melodic line, how individual tones are strung together to create a musical phrase. I then extend my awareness to the development of my entire solo. That solo exists within the context of the larger piece. Is my solo at the beginning, middle, or end of the piece? Does my solo function as an invitation to the listener, a further development of materials already introduced, or is it climactic, a dramatic summation of everything that's gone before?

My awareness extends further to the arc of the set or concert as a whole. Again, are we at the beginning, the middle, or the end of the concert? Within the arc of the entire evening, what is needed from me, more energy or less? Does this piece stand as an introduction, a gentle interlude, or the dramatic peak of the entire concert? What else can I sense in the moment?

Art: Can I relax enough to sense the audience, that they're getting bored or that they need a little more information or they need things to calm down? And then can I sense the environment? If the windows are open, I can see nature, and sometimes I can see my grandparents, people who have gone before me, Miles Davis. I'm playing my piece, but the scope starts getting larger.

Mark: I'm thinking about when we played after 9/11, when the energy in the room was so palpable. And do you remember when we played in Sonoma right after those terrible fires?

Art: And we invited the audience to play with us, which was really strong. It isn't just our little concert, it's part of the whole world. Not to overstate this, but often musicians are focused only on the details. Did they follow the chord progression? Did they get it right? But did you also remember to place some nice tones for your mom? Did you notice that it's windy outside? If you don't hyper-focus, you can realize that you're part of something bigger.

Band within a Band (Orchestration)

Sometimes you can be more productive by not doing than by doing, by making space for others to play rather than by driving forward on your own. Stopping or resting allows different possibilities to emerge. For example, contained within any quintet are five factorial subgroups: five possible solos, ten possible duos, ten trios and five quartets. In a jazz quintet comprised of voice, saxophone, piano, bass, and drums the various bands within the band are as follows:

Duos:
1) voice and saxophone
2) voice and piano
3) voice and bass
4) voice and drums
5) saxophone and piano
6) saxophone and bass
7) saxophone and drums (my favorite)
8) piano and bass
9) piano and drums
10) bass and drums

Trios:
1) piano, bass, and drums
2) saxophone, bass, and drums
3) saxophone, piano, and drums
4) saxophone, piano, and bass
5) voice, bass, and drums
6) voice, piano, and drums
7) voice, piano, and bass
8) voice, saxophone, and drums
9) voice, saxophone, and bass
10) voice, saxophone, and piano

Quartets:
1) voice, saxophone, piano, and bass
2) voice, saxophone, piano, and drums
3) voice, saxophone, bass, and drums
4) voice, piano, bass, and drums
5) saxophone, piano, bass, and drums

We also have a range of relationships within each subgroup. For example, a piano/saxophone duo offers three permutations: a saxophone solo with piano accompaniment, a piano solo with saxophone accompaniment, or saxophone and piano in counterpoint. Either player can also accompany by resting—moments when one person plays and the other listens. By featuring different combinations of instruments, we can create sonic variety within the ensemble. A quintet performance is potentially a concert of twenty-five different bands, assuming that the players are sometimes willing to rest.

Contributing Silence

Art: Keeping up with the pulse of the world or the motion of the planet— it's hard for people resist that. They think, "I've got to keep this thing going."

Mark: And culturally there's an insistence on productivity. We feel that we've got to be productive all the time, every single moment.

Art: But you are also being productive by receiving the world. You are being productive through your awareness. In fact, you're contributing a lot by being a witness, and by celebrating, noticing what's going on around you. If I'm silent, I'm contributing my silence.

In a workshop at the School for Improvisational Music, I told the students that there's no reason to play when you're unsure about what to contribute, when it's not time yet, and that it's fine to listen or wait until you hear your contribution. I was playing in a trio with a bass player and trumpet player. The bass player and I started together, but the trumpet player didn't play anything for the first three minutes. That was amazing. She entered when the piece really needed the trumpet, and her first statement was wonderful. She later took a long, well-developed unaccompanied solo, and we ended the piece briefly, all together.

When I asked how that was for her, she said that it was the most comfortable she had ever felt performing, and the most natural she had ever felt on stage in front of people. She allowed herself to be, rather than feeling like she had to produce something. She felt, "I'm here, I have my perspective, here are the listeners, here's the music playing, and here's my part." She felt like a regular person instead of whatever uncomfortable thing people usually feel in that position.

For me, it's really important not to feel self-conscious and awkward. What I love most is when I just feel regular, like a plant or a bird, just in the space, and I don't have to be smart or talented or witty or anything; I can just be.

Exercise: Solos from Stillness

In this exercise, we create three four-minute solo pieces in this order:

1) For four minutes the soloist does nothing. The soloist may stand, sit, or lie down.
2) During the second round, the soloist is allowed one gesture, movement, or statement sometime during the allotted four minutes—just one. For the rest of the time, the soloist practices stillness.
3) During the third round, the soloist may allow their gesture to open outward into a piece that develops over the four-minute time frame.

Art: The three stages are beingness, gesture arising, gesture leading onward. We try to learn how to be in a space/time without putting on a show—to simply be and let an action arise from stillness. How did that feel to the performer? What did the audience sense? Did the solo feel long, short, uncomfortable, relaxing, nervous? Did the gesture feel authentic, or did the soloist try to do something really cool or clever? Did it seem connected or disconnected with the silence? How did it feel when the action was early or late in the time span, or when the gesture was large or small? We are trying to learn how to be comfortable with the stillness of just being and allow the piece to emerge from that.

Chapter 7

Structured Improvisation

The music we play ranges from open improvisation with no preset content or form, to pieces that feature a single musical element—a written melody, scale, or harmonic structure—all the way to carefully notated music that resembles classical composition more than jazz. In between, we've developed a variety of strategies that help us generate content and form.

We've discovered that even a little bit of prearranged material can help us sustain our creative energies over the course of an entire evening by providing a musical "seed syllable," a simple but potent idea that hints at a sonic universe that we can explore. These are uncomplicated creative suggestions: a title, motif, scale, pitch set, structure, or musical concept to spark the imagination. Here are a few of these structures, ranging from minimal to more complex.

Title Pieces

Title pieces consist of a title only. A good title suggests a direction, a mood, or a topic for investigation. Here are a few of the titles we've explored in concert:

- She's Nice to Animals
- Jocular Josephine
- A Solid Thing Begins to Fall Apart and is Saved by Bob
- Lost

- Stay There Until I Get Back
- Luscious Cream
- Sure, I'll Be Fine in that Chair
- Outbursts and Soothing
- The Tide's Doom
- Simple, Easy, and Fun
- Bad Dudes
- Perpetual Goodness
- Frost on the Window
- Just Keep Filling That Up with Different Things
- Hanging Lanterns

Short Worlds

In Short Worlds, we choose a musical focus and explore it. Each exploration is concise, lasting only a minute or two. This is similar to the "Two Lists" exercise in Chapter 3.

- dense/sparse
- steady/erratic
- toy instruments
- words only
- two different tempos at the same time
- bitonality (two different keys at the same time)
- loud/soft
- alternation (never play together)
- counterpoint (play contrasting ideas at the same time)
- non-traditional sounds
- scales (move by step)
- arpeggios (move by leap)

Germs

These are motifs or short melodic ideas that we prepare ahead of time and then explore in concert. Germs are infused with musical possibility and infect the improvisation with creative energy.

Whippets

Whippets are germs that are meant to be played very fast.

Tone Rows

As in classical composition, a tone row includes all twelve tones in the chromatic scale, set in any order. We improvise on the row following (more or less) the traditional format developed by the composer Arnold Schoenberg. The tones in the row are numbered 1–12. They can be played one at a time or in combination, but the entire series has to be completed before you return to any of the previous tones. The rhythm and phrasing are improvised. We might also improvise loosely on the row, improvising a "twelve tone-ish" piece that has no tonal center but does not strictly follow this form.

1. Single tones or groups of tones can be repeated before moving through the rest of the row.
2. Notes can be played in any octave.
3. For chordal instruments like piano and guitar, notes can be grouped together into chords. For example, the pianist can create chords by playing three tones at a time: 1+2+3, 4+5+6, 7+8+9, 10+11+12. These non-standard chords are useful in improvisation because they don't create harmonic expectation. That is, no tonal center or key is established, and one chord doesn't seem to lead directly to another.
4. Sections of the row can be repeated one note at a time as riffs or background parts: 1,2,3, 1,2,3, 1,2,3, 4,5, 4,5, 4,5, etc.
5. The row can be played four different ways: original (as written), retrograde (backwards), or as an inversion (upside down. An inversion is a mirror image of the row. For example, in Row #1 below, instead of going up four steps from D to G, the inversion would begin by going down four steps from D to A.) Finally, the row can be played as a retrograde inversion (upside down and backwards). Because these strict variations are difficult to execute on the fly, they are most useful in improvisation if you write them down.

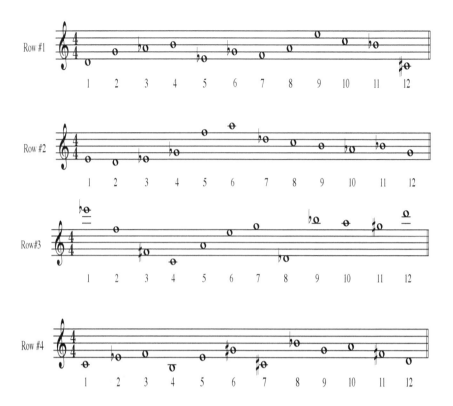

Discussed Things

These are pieces based on groups of notes (pitch sets) that we use in various ways. The notes and the order in which they are played are given, but other aspects of the performance (rhythm, rests, dynamics, phrasing, range, etc.) are improvised. This allows us to come to quick agreement about one of the most challenging aspects of improvisation—which notes will we use?

Discussed Thing A

1. Expose and explore themes in order.
2. Mix themes.
3. Touch briefly on each theme to conclude.

Discussed Thing B

1. Expose and explore themes in order.
2. Play themes in order, then play in the style of a fugue. (The theme is staggered. As one person begins to play the theme, the other waits, and then begins to play the theme a beat or two later.)
3. Mix themes.

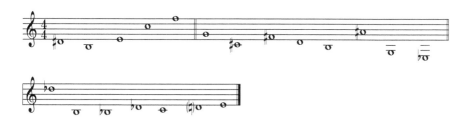

Discussed Thing C

1. Play themes in reverse order.
2. Solos: the accompanist uses the given notes, the soloist improvises freely.
3. Play themes in order: forward, backward, backward, forward.

Menu Pieces

A menu piece contains a set of composed musical ideas or motifs that anyone can play at any time, in any combination or order. One example is Art's composition "Azmoxic Libula #1."

"Azmoxic Libula #1" Instructions

1. Play melody three times: 1) as written, 2) at different speeds, 3) as a fugue.
2. Accompanist plays part B as written, soloist improvises freely.
3. Play any of the three lines as many times as you want to, in any order, at any tempo. Fragment, repeat, play retrograde, etc. When bar lines are absent, meter is freely interpreted.
4. Conclusion: Play as written.

Azmoxic Libula #1

Art Lande

Poetry Music

A poem can evoke a feeling or mood and provide inspiration for an improvisation. We can illustrate the words of the poem in sound or use it as an introduction to a free-standing, improvised piece.

Head Charts

Art has written over 400 pieces of music that, true to the traditional jazz format, include melodies, chord changes, and other written elements such as bass lines, solo sections, and written background parts as structures for improvisation.

Fully Notated Pieces

We sometimes play pieces that involve no improvisation at all, or that may be used as an introduction, transition, or springboard to open improvisation. Examples include Art's carefully rendered "Penances." These are like short classical works.

Coda

All of these forms are prompts that create focus by limiting what can happen in the music, at least in the beginning. If a title piece is called "Luscious Cream," only lusciously creamy sounds are invited in. A germ grows according to its musical genetic code until we decide to "cure" the music and move on, or until it meets its own demise. If no form is established ahead of time, both form and content become part of our improvisational journey. The key, as always, is awareness. What is this piece about? What is this section about? Can I "hear forward" to what happens next?

Art: Sometimes our pieces have a specific focus and are quite short. They expose an area and come to conclusion without development. They are miniatures about one thing. It's satisfying to tell about something clearly and succinctly. We listen for a suitable ending.

The band Kneebody will sometimes play a long, complex piece with lots of sections, followed by a 45-second piece that is pretty much through-composed (completely written), a little jewel, a visit.

In order to play a short, improvised piece, the group has to be comfortable with ending. We have to go into it and then let it go. That's it. Enough. OK as it stands. If we get greedy, indulgent, or judgmental— that is, if we go on because we're afraid that it isn't good enough—we can't end. And if we bypass the obvious ending, a satisfying exit may not appear. The Russian composer Nicolas Slonimsky felt that once the listener is able to grasp the nature of a piece, this ended its freshness, so he tried ending the piece before the listener's concept had time to form. He created 5-second or 7-second pieces that end before we know what's going on.

Chapter 8

Pulling the Plug on Perfection

This play is an affirmation of life—not an attempt to bring order out of chaos nor to suggest improvements in creation, but simply a way of waking up to the very life we are living, which is so excellent once one gets one's mind and one's desires out of its way.
— John Cage (1961, p. 12)

Perfectionism can be paralyzing in improvisation. We all want to play well, to play perfectly in tune, to execute every phrase with perfect integrity, but perfection is not the goal in improvisation. The goal, as Art says, "is to liberate ourselves and our friends so we can be free from right and wrong, good and bad, and do other things with our energy."

We might see perfectionism as the pursuit of excellence, the driving force behind an indomitable work ethic. But perfectionism is really an expression of ego, an attitude of perpetual dissatisfaction dressed up as virtue. Ego tells us, "This isn't good enough. I deserve better." But as the pianist Michael Jefry Stevens says, "The ego is not a reliable ally in music making" (Stevens, 2008).

Because perfectionism rejects what is, the cure for perfectionism is gratitude for what we are given: the time to listen, imagine, and create together. The great jazz tenor saxophonist Sonny Rollins (2015) proclaimed, "Enjoy music and be a good person. Then you have it all." He didn't mention perfect playing. When we relax our perfectionism, we can participate fully in whatever happens rather than criticize or give up when things don't work out. Imperfection isn't a problem. Imperfection is the path.

Art: You give yourself this idealized version of how things are supposed to go, and then when it doesn't go that way, you're angry and frustrated. So why set up disappointment? That doesn't mean that you can't have a concept, but so what if it doesn't happen the way you planned? Just go along with what does happen and get the experience, be open to the adventure. It might be just as good or better than what you originally conceived. I didn't get to San Francisco to play my gig, but I did end up in Detroit and I got to see the Tigers play. Especially in highly improvised music, if we get attached to a concept of how things should go, we create tension and set up disappointment in ourselves and the people we play with.

Mark: The psychologist and meditation master Tara Brach (2003; 2013) teaches that we don't have to believe everything we think, that we can let go of constricting thoughts that make our world smaller. If you think, "This music is annoying," or even, "This music is going to be beautiful," that's a concept. You've shrunk your world; you've put limitations on the music.

Art: It's nice to relax the muscle that worries about where the music is going, and just say, "OK, this is how it is." This doesn't mean that you can't make choices about how to work with it, but people are playing what they feel and what they hear. In that moment, there's nothing to do, nothing to fight about. The other approach is a hell realm. Can you imagine a control freak trying to play in our band?

Wabi-Sabi

In the Japanese classical arts, the term *wabi-sabi* refers to an aesthetic and way of life that celebrates modesty, earthiness, and unpretentiousness. From the wabi-sabi point of view, creativity is a natural but imperfect process that celebrates simplicity, asymmetry, austerity, and freedom from habit and convention. Wabi-sabi rejects rigid formality and cultivates a sense of appreciation for the world as it is: a broken teacup skillfully repaired, the rough glaze and imperfect shape of a raku pot, the breathy tone of a shakuhachi flute, as unrefined and natural as wind through a bamboo grove.

According to Leonard Koren (1994), wabi-sabi works are "one-of-a kind, personal, intuitive, idiosyncratic, and present-oriented" (p. 26). Many of these same characteristics are found in improvisation. When the music is spontaneous, the result may sound unpolished but also fresh and unpredictable. Imperfection can be a sign of authenticity, a reflection of natural processes and creative flow. When the music challenges our aesthetic expectations in a provocative way, improvisers might praise the work for its abstraction, strangeness, or deep sense of mystery.

Art: A student was just here for her lesson, and she recently got the duo record "Sioux County" with Pete Sommer and me.[1] The first piece is beautiful, and the first note that I chose on my solo was the most unlikely, even for me! I don't know how I had the guts to play it so strong to start. It's in C major and I don't remember what note it was, but I wanted to hear what would happen—and she said it woke her up. OK! Now what, because you've said that?

Mark: I'm interested in the idea of naturalness, how things sometimes sound better when they're not perfect, when we're not trying so hard.

Art: Instead of perfect posture and effort and trying, sometimes I consciously do the opposite. I take away the control mechanism of both my brain and my body. I let my muscles relax and I let my brain sag, just to see what plays. I'm not trying to play bad, I just kind of pull the plug on perfection.

I might allow in random thoughts that might otherwise be a distraction. If I start singing third grade roll call ("Mary Bishop, David Lewis, Calvin Smith, are you here?"), it's because it came up and I didn't censor it. I didn't think of it to try to be weird, and I'm not trying to cause anything. It's just, there it was: I start to sing these names. What does this

---

[1] Peter Sommer is a saxophonist and Associate Professor of Music at Colorado State University.

have to do with anything? Well, I'm going to let it in and find out. I relax the muscles of the brain and the body and then see what comes up.

Mark: There's simplicity in not trying, not overdoing. Sometimes when people try to make something happen, it doesn't work so well.

Art: Because it's contrived. When you're trying to cause the effect rather than just allowing it, that's different. I don't like contrivance in films—when they put something in just for shock value, or they're trying to be clever or different, or trying to manipulate me with a message.

Mark: Or they're trying to be artsy...

Art: Or modern—whatever it is. But if the thing just comes up, there's innocence in it. There's innocence rather than wanting people to notice me, wanting to affect the whole thing. Something comes up and I allow it in.

Mark: That sense of innocence or "not trying" allows us to be curious and playful.

Art: When you're intrigued by something from an organic, almost childlike curiosity, you're not manipulating other people and you're not manipulating the music, you're just allowing it so it can exist as part of the music. I don't like the identity of "musician" if it means that I have to play well on my best instrument all of the time. I can also tell a story, read a poem, or make a word piece.

Failure

In an improvisation, the vocalist sings a high "D," piercing in its clarity and precision, and I try to match it with my soprano saxophone. Instead, I hit a "C#," one half step below them. The result is dissonant and a little disconcerting, but neither the audience nor the other musicians know (or care) what my intention was. Did I make a mistake? Is this failure? The answer depends on my frame of mind.

Listening to the relationship of these two notes, I have several options. I could resolve my note by quickly matching theirs and immediately eliminate any feelings of discomfort or uncertainty. I could construct a melodic flourish that connects my note with theirs by resolving to a less disruptive interval, like a third or a sixth. Or, I could revel in the dissonance, taking pleasure in the spiciness that our tones create together. But if I label this event a "mistake" or think of it as failure, I have encapsulated my experience in a way that constricts creative possibility and makes the way forward more difficult.

Art: The idea is not to accept failure. In basketball, the Warriors do it all the time. Part of the reason they succeed is that they don't quit. They might commit a bunch of turnovers, but they end up with a dunk. They score, but that process includes all the mistakes that they made. They're having fun and they're being warriors, literally. I feel that in the music. I'm not willing to accept that what we're doing is going to fail. It's not going to fail for me; I'm going to be an alchemist. Somehow, I'm going to turn this into gold.

Creativity is working with what actually happens. It's not about making something new, because everything on the planet has already been done. If we invite a grouchy person to our party, we can have fun if we work with them in an interesting, joyful, and good-spirited way. We have playfulness, clear intention, and imagination. We just have to avoid getting waylaid by this so-called "miss" or "failure," not having a pleasant result right away. It doesn't mean that you can't notice that you're a half step lower, it's that there's nothing wrong with that. Even though it might be a surprise to hear a minor second when you thought you were going to hear a unison, it can work because that's what you did.

And then there are times when we know full well what the "right" note is, but we choose not to play it. So, both your knowledge and your ignorance can be useful. I don't think they're that different. A perfectionist might say that there is a huge difference, but I think you don't have to know everything. It's OK not to be good at it all, all the time. If I don't hear the chord right, then what I juxtapose could be pretty interesting.

We're like a bunch of four-year-olds. We just want to be with our friends, right? So, when you hit a note, I want to find it. But it might be two and a half octaves away and not something that I can even imagine on my melodica, so I'll leap up toward you and if you hold, I'll eventually find you. If you move, then we're playing chase.

It's innocent and childlike, wanting to be together, and yet I'm almost happier when I miss and have to go dribbling down or up, so my inquiry becomes my melody. All of the notes leading to the one you're searching for is not failure. It's your pathway.

Mark: There is value in wandering; you don't have to follow your GPS all the time. If you focus only on your destination, on perfection, you'll miss a lot along the way.

Art: If you're embracing all of it, then there are no mistakes. What I hear is the whole thing. But if I think, "My part doesn't fit with that part," then there's a problem. Either you're delighted by that problem, which means that you try to fix the note you played, or you decide that the note sounds kind of neat, and maybe you'll make more of them on purpose. You can change your perspective really quickly. It's about unity and diversity, which I think is one of the main games in town. Is it all one, or are there things that are bouncing off each other? I'm not scared of being drawn into the all, where there's no differentiation. There's just resting in being-ness, which has its own organic alternation between being everything and being a thing. It's the same in the music.

Mark: As we said earlier, this doesn't mean that we shouldn't think critically about what we're doing. There are often ways to make the music clearer and more enjoyable for everyone, things that we can be aware of and practice. At the jam session the other night, I noticed that a lot of the improvisers were relying on imitation. Of course, imitation is one possibility, but that's all they were doing—copying what somebody else was playing rather than offering their own point of view. It was frustrating. There were some really good musicians on stage, and I wanted to hear what they had to say. It might have been more interesting if someone had added something that wasn't already there.

Art: If you play long tones and I think the part needs more fullness, I might join you. I like thickening. If the piano and the drums are doing something together, it can have more substance and weight, but I'm not imitating, I'm joining. It can be frustrating if the imitation is linear, one person constantly repeating what another person plays.

I call it first and second listening. First listening is a reaction. I say, "Look, there's a chair." and you say, "Yes, there's a chair." Children do that. All beginning improvisers do that. They're trying to be nice. It means that they heard you, but they haven't heard their own part.

Second listening is a response to what you hear. I say, "There's a chair," and you say, "I'm tired, I think I'll sit down." That's a response, not a reaction, and it moves the conversation forward. I've noticed also that beginners tend to start tentatively. They're afraid to do something definitive. Those things work together. They're afraid to do something definitive because they think they have to fit in. They don't respond, they react. If one person is playing something percussive, then they think they have to do that rather than respond to it. They're being careful, trying to fit in.

Mark: To respond effectively, sometimes you have to take a risk. Being overly cautious or trying too hard to be perfect can undermine our ability to take that risk, to be clear and direct when communicating a point of view, rather than constantly worrying about whether you're right or wrong.

Chapter 9

Is Music A Language?

In his book *Improvisation*, Derek Bailey (1993) describes two approaches to improvised music: idiomatic improvisation, which is created according to the guidelines of a particular tradition or genre, and non-idiomatic improvisation, which is free from stylistic constraints.

Idiomatic improvisation encompasses jazz, blues, rock, Flamenco, Indian classical music, early European classical music, and many other styles. Some improvisers make their home within a tradition; others follow a less restrictive path. There are many ways to make music. The question is, what is the best way for you to tell your story?

Art: What interests me today is language—musical language and how it can facilitate or hinder what we do.

Mark: How are you defining "musical language?"

Art: The languages that students might learn in music schools—jazz or classical language and other styles like bluegrass or the blues. Some musicians won't play anything that they haven't already learned. They master a particular style and then when they improvise, language matters too much to them or they get too good at it. On the other hand, if you imagine that you could be original, that none of it is derivative, that's also a problem. People get frustrated because either they're trying to copy a certain style, or they're trying not to, and both are uncomfortable. So, is musical language useful or is it debilitating?

Mark: There's the old cliché: "You have to know the rules before you can break them." You have to learn the language—the musical grammar, syntax, and vocabulary—before you can try anything different or creative. I don't believe that, but how do you think about it?

Art: Somebody mentioned that Picasso learned how to do everything perfectly, and then he wanted to paint like a two-year-old, which is exactly how it feels to me. I know different styles and the specifics of theory, the principles of overtones, and how to finger everything, but I hardly use the conventions or defy them. Even when I'm supposed to use the language that fits, I might play the thing that doesn't fit.

Hybridization

Art: I've been thinking about musical languages from different parts of the world and how important they've been to me—traveling to Europe and meeting Turkish people and Romanian people and North Africans and West Africans and Nguyên Lê, who was born in Vietnam. All these different rhythms and scales and sounds and inflections and instruments started showing up in the palette of what I wanted to play or what I needed to hear. Not in a sectarian way; I don't know their music the way they do. It's about knowing different people from different places and points of view. That affects your sense of the music.

Mark: We're talking about hybridization—not mastering a different language in its purest sense but mixing influences in a musical way. The band Oregon was like that, with Collin Wolcott playing tabla and sitar, Ralph Towner on classical guitar, Paul McCandless improvising on oboe, and Glen Moore on bass. Different instruments and stylistic ideas from different traditions can come together in new ways. The rapper Nas sampled Carl Orff's Carmina Burana in "Hate Me Now," Kool Keith incorporated Bartok's second violin concerto in "Blue Flowers," and contemporary classical composers like Anna Thorvaldsdottir ("In Light of Air") and Mason Bates ("Mothership") incorporate electronics with their orchestral music. When you hear something you like, how can you not be influenced by it? You are what you hear. I'm in favor of taking up different influences as long as we're respectful about where they come from, and as long as we don't claim to be something we're not.

Art: I don't want to live my life in music saying, "Don't do that. It isn't part of the tradition." I love Bulgarian music, but I shouldn't play it because I don't live in Bulgaria? You've got to let it all in and let it all out.

Poetry, Painting, and Movement

Mark: When you work with students who aren't focusing on a particular language or tradition like jazz, what do you have them do?

Art: I think the cross-fertilization of dance and speech, and even spatial relationships are really helpful. They're fun to do and they humanize the music. I'll draw a spatial idea on the board—here's a swirl, and here's a dot—and then ask the students to play that in a linear way. This brings in more life than just writing something out in musical notation. You just play shapes. Ways of combining drawing, speaking, and movement are good because these are the sources of the music. When I read written music, I also want to see it as shapes, spaces, and densities, not only as individual notes.

Sound is related to movement. At the University of Colorado, I send the drummers out into the courtyard. I tell them to have their sticks in their hands and move however they want for 10 minutes, and then come in and go to the drum set and keep doing the same thing. These are the motions that are satisfying to them, and interesting to them, that have nothing to do with what they learned on the drums. These are dance movements, an organic sense of dancing. Then what they play is much more interesting and rhythmically alive than the routinized drum stuff that they practice. There was one drummer—he was really good, a jazz and rock superstar—but his playing was so stiff that it didn't feel fun to play with him or listen to him. I had to do that kind of exercise with him a lot, and wow, it humanized his rhythm.

Mark: These are your own rhythms, the rhythms of your own body.

Art: Again, it's so organic and basic. You can't move like somebody else. You've got to move how you move. Look at ball players, how different everybody looks on a basketball court. They don't all move the same way. Nobody moves like Jokic, the Nugget's center, the way he lumbers. I think rhythm is part of that, what your metabolism is like and whether you're round or angular. All these things are expressions of your animal nature. You can't just learn the rhythms of other people and other cultures. You have to be able to find your own rhythms.

You also have to find the beauty of motion within rhythm and know that there are different rhythms within the pulse (the steady beat). What's the difference between music when it's pulsing, and music that isn't pulsing? Like most things in the world, water doesn't pulse, the air doesn't pulse, and "WE. DO. NOT. TALK. LIKE. THIS. We don't talk just in quarter notes and eighth notes. We need to be able to see the connection between the straightened-out pulsing of rhythm and motion that is related but not right in the pulse.

Most of the music that you hear on the radio is pulsing. Sometimes people don't know how to take a solo that isn't in the pulse, or how to create a part or a piece that has movement but doesn't pulse, or how to change from pulsing to non-pulsing at any moment. It's very specific to your own sense of shape and movement.

Affirming Your Sense of the World

Art: But sound is the essence. Just as you know the difference between Sonny Rollins and Ben Webster right away, it's not what they're playing; it's how they're playing and how the instrument sounds to them. It's like people's voices—you can recognize them right away. This, again, is affirming your own sense of the world rather than being imitative.

It's also about connection with the earth. In Denney Goodhew's[1] beginning improvisation class at Cornish, the students began by playing just one note, and they had to get it from the earth. It was all about legs and connecting your feet to the ground and pushing and standing up, getting the lower half of your body to play, not just the hands. I've been

---

[1] Denney Goodhew is a saxophonist, drummer, painter and improviser from Seattle, WA.

working on that with pianists a lot, and drummers. Things grow from roots, they don't grow from the top down. Nothing works that way. And yes, feeling your gut and your core and your center. Otherwise, everything is on the surface and you won't get a good sound. Watch a great tennis player prepare to receive a serve, or Nolan Arenado playing third base. They're like a tiger getting ready to pounce.

The hand at the piano or the drums is the last thing to touch the instrument. It's not where the sound emanates from. If you just grab, it's all about result instead of process. When I go to reach for this pen, I have to push from my right foot in order to get it. I can't reach it just with my hand. But you see people trying to play the piano that way– just fingers pushing buttons like they're texting.

Mark: To return to our original question: Is music a language that we need to learn in order to improvise, or can we just rely on our personal experience?

Art: I think it's like everything we've talked about; it's both/and. You have to learn the rules, but music is not just about right and wrong. You have to practice being expressive and creative. You can play the feeling of the blues while you learn the relationship of the I and the IV chords. You can learn the form of the blues while you experiment with different rhythms or weird intervals. The essence of the music is important, and the essence can get lost in the details. Some people think, "Well, now I know how to do it and other people think I'm good, so that's that." Okay, but that's not everything.

Chapter 10

Jazz Improvisation

Jazz is a balance of what we are given and what we give back. What we are given is a rich and complex musical tradition with roots in African American history and branches that extend through other cultures and musical styles. What we give back is our own story, our first-person perspective on the jazz tradition and what we want to bring forward from the past into the present.

For students of jazz, the learning curve is steep. The music requires substantial instrumental or vocal proficiency, a comprehensive understanding of music theory and jazz history, and most important, a lifelong dedication to *praxis*—embodied listening and playing. For musicians interested in learning to play jazz, resources abound in the form of books, classes, play-along recordings, and software. The following is a brief introduction to some of the ingredients of jazz improvisation, and for those who are already proficient a few suggestions about how you can explore the territory beyond these basic concepts.

First, an important caveat: It isn't possible to learn jazz from a book or a set of concepts alone. We learn by listening to live performances and recordings of accomplished players, jazz masters who have made the music their own. That said, these elements are an important part of a daily practice routine, a good place to begin.

Jazz Basics

Choose a composition from the jazz repertoire—a jazz standard, blues or other work—and begin to familiarize yourself with these essential components of the piece.

1. The melody. If the song has words, learn them as a guide to phrasing and articulation.
2. Bass notes. Be able to sing and play the root (the lowest tone) of each chord in the progression.
3. Chord functions: Study the relationships of the chords within keys or other groupings.
4. Chord tones. Be able to play all of the notes of each chord. For example, a C7b9 chord is a combination of the tones C, E, G, Bb & Db, called the root, third, fifth, seventh and ninth. This is the "vertical" expression of the harmony.
5. Lead lines. Learn how the third and seventh of each chord (E and Bb in the example above) flow smoothly to the third and seventh of the following chord. This is the "horizontal" expression of the harmony.
6. Chord scales. Individual chords or groups of chords often suggest the use of certain compatible scales or modes.
7. Other considerations: Work with motifs, sequences (patterns), chord substitutions, phrasing, and the ability to play outside of the given harmonic context.
8. Listen to how accomplished jazz musicians work with all of the above, including (and perhaps most important) the rhythmic feel of the music. Ultimately, jazz is not about *what* you play; it's about *how* you play.

Jazz music is complex and technically demanding. It takes years to master all of the elements involved. Our challenge is to bring personal expression into relationship with theory and technique, "like two arrows meeting in mid-air" (Suzuki, 1999, p. 191).

A Word About Practicing, Learning, and Growing

According to W.A. Mathieu (1992) all musicians, no matter what style or genre they want to represent, need to develop in four essential areas: instrumental or vocal technique, music theory, ear training, and self-expression. We all have strengths and weaknesses in each of these domains. Our task is to celebrate our strengths while working to improve our skills in other areas.

Good technique, a solid understanding of music theory and history, and the ability to hear what's happening as the music plays are tools that enable us to be expressive and articulate. Good musicianship allows us to transform our being into music without any part of us getting lost in translation. Practicing is a lifelong process of removing obstacles to honest music making—playing what you hear and hearing what you play. We think of practicing as a cyclical process that includes the following steps:

1. Practice. Work on the essentials, including scales, arpeggios, intervals, fingerings, chords and chord progressions, intonation, motivic development, solfeggio, rhythm, meter, repertoire, and the list goes on. Efficient practicing often involves working diligently with one small piece of the puzzle, not everything all at once. If you don't know what to practice or how to practice, work with an experienced and trustworthy teacher.
2. Play. Focus on expression, imagination, and listening. Notice what works and what needs further attention. Bookmark your observations for later reference.
3. Practice. Work on what you noticed. If you struggle in a particular key, work on that. If you have difficulty identifying intervals or hearing chord qualities, work on ear training. If your time is a little shaky, slow down and work on rhythmic

precision. Video and live recordings of your playing can be very helpful in identifying areas that need work.

4. Play. Don't worry about any of the above. Trust that whatever you've been practicing will be incorporated organically into your playing over time. Just play, then repeat the cycle of practice and play.

Mixing these steps creates problems. Practicing is a narrowly focused, analytical discipline. Playing is intuitive, open-ended, and expressive.

Jazz masters like Louis Armstrong, Duke Ellington, Charlie Parker, Miles Davis and John Coltrane were steeped in the jazz tradition. Their creativity was grounded in the wisdom of their musical elders. Then they added something new—a fresh point of view, a personal variation on conventional practice that transformed the music and created new directions for the rest of us to explore. Of course, we can't all contribute on the level of Miles Davis or John Coltrane, but these innovative musicians provide a model for how we can engage with this complex and challenging music. To play jazz, we need to bring the technical, traditional, and personal points of view into creative accord.

Art: The jazz pianist Jason Moran is doing all kinds of interesting things with the history of the music. He's not imitating the old way; he's using traditional elements in a new way, integrating the history with contemporary music, blurring the line.

Mark: In the music of contemporary players like Ravi Coltrane (saxophone), Ralph Alessi (trumpet) and pianists Myra Melford and Fred Hersch, we hear the essence of the tradition. But they express themselves in an unmistakably personal way through both their playing and their writing. Jazz music is vital and alive with so many great young players coming up, but I wonder about jazz education programs that seem to emphasize tradition at the expense of self-expression. We've seen it at different universities. Students are taught to memorize licks and ii–V formulas or, as Fred Hersch puts it, to learn "widgets" so they can navigate complicated chord progressions. For the really great players, tradition is the foundation, but it isn't prescriptive or formulaic.

Art: Students who want to play jazz have to know all aspects of the music—bass lines, lead lines, chords and chord scales, form, swing feel, melody, and so on. But there's danger in doing the neoclassical thing only. It can end up sounding really stuffy and pedantic, like they're trying to teach us something instead of really playing. Students listen to classic jazz and they work hard on it, and then they want to show what they've learned and that they're good at it. Then the bass player and the piano player and the drummer sound like "Music Minus One." The drummer's going "ding-ding-a-ding," and the bass player is walking, and the piano player is playing all the chords, all the time. They think, "I want to be good, like Miles in 1952," but a lot has happened since then.

It's important to understand the history, but it's also important to realize that we have more possibilities for individual and group creativity now. The bass doesn't always have to walk, and the drums don't always have to keep a beat. The piano player doesn't always have to play the chords, and horn players can be responsible for more than just the melody. The point is to tell the story of the piece in different ways so it's not the same exact thing every time.

Playing jazz, there are lots of different things you can do, but there's nothing you have to do. Students think that there is something they have to do based on what they've studied, and so they do all that. And when all of them are doing all that, the sound world is not intriguing and the soloist has no freedom to explore.

I think there's an illusion that you always have to play because people come from reading rather than listening. When they see a chord, they think they have to play it. I play a quarter of the chords I see, maybe fewer, or maybe even none. Whether it's the sound of your whole band or the instruments you choose and how you choose to play them, we want to be selective. We have to get past the traditional roles, how they're usually set.

Mark: So, we're not just a collection of individuals fulfilling our traditional roles; the band is a creative organism working together with the soloist, exploring different ways of playing the music.

Art: When I accompany you, I can contribute movement to your solo in a way that doesn't interrupt what you're saying. I listen for your breath, and I listen for tones. When you play a long tone, which is one of the reasons I love to play with you, I can harmonize that long tone from the top down, any kind of weird voicing, using the tone that you showed me. Students aren't listening to specifics partly because they don't know their pitches well enough, but partly because they're too busy doing all that other stuff.

Mark: It's the same with horn players. When we see a chord symbol, we're tempted to play all of the possible permutations of that chord, scales, and arpeggios. It takes confidence to leave space, to play phrases rather than filling every bar with notes.

Art: I might decide to stop playing because the music doesn't need me, or I see that it would be nice to build energy, or come in on the bridge only. Or I'll play only two-note chords, providing a texture that the soloist can work with. I don't use both hands and all ten fingers very often. Why? Because there are three or four or six other people playing too. Why does the music need me to do that? It all depends on what the soloist is up to.

I might link with other people who are suggesting a dynamic level or a rhythmic inflection that will last for a while. I might play something that's missing: if there are no high insects, I might do a little of that, but it doesn't get in the way of anything; it's insects flying in the sky. Or I might double a bass part that's kind of interesting and sustain that for a while or harmonize with it.

The Song is More Than Just Your Part

Art: Another issue for some students is that if they're having trouble maintaining the form, especially when the form is complicated, the only way they keep track is by playing everything. If they rest, they get lost, so they play in order not to get lost. They're keeping track through action. If everybody is doing that, that's a lot of playing! Students have to learn to embody and internalize the form so they can give more of their attention to listening.

Mark: When you're teaching students how to keep track of the form, what do you have them do?

Art: Again, every jazz musician should know all parts of the music— melody, harmony, and rhythm. The drummer Paul Romaine[1] teaches his students to sing the melody—and not only that, to sing the melody while playing the drums. The song is not just your part; it's all the parts. And the more you embody all the parts, they're there for you even when nobody is playing them.

Whenever we notice that there's an issue, we find a way to work on it. If there's a three-bar phrase and we keep messing it up, we work on that. You can write down the bar structure and count it on your fingers like they do in Indian music. If the piano solo is too busy, I'll ask the piano player to play a maximum of four times during eight bars, or I'll ask them to play short, one- or two-bar phrases with the rest only breathing, just to get used to another parameter besides all those notes.

There doesn't have to be a tremendous divide between open improvisation and playing a song. We don't have to play the typical four-bar drum intro, the head played twice, each person soloing starting with the horns and ending with the drums, trading fours, playing the out-head and maybe a coda (but probably not) or a tag ending that goes on and on forever. I don't want to do "jazz museum" where there's no creation going on and we just do it by the book. Not that there's anything wrong with that, but it doesn't interest me.

We have different ways of working with form. For example, it enlivens the band when the introduction is freely created. It can be just one person, or it can be a duet. If the piece is "Early Autumn," the bass and horn can play how it feels to be early autumn. I might read a poem so we can get into what I would call the real content of the piece. The introduction sets the mood and gets you into the heart of the piece without all of the details.

---

[1] Paul Romaine is a jazz drummer, faculty member at the University of Colorado, Boulder, and founder of Colorado Conservatory for the Jazz Arts.

What if you play the head (the melody) three times or like Miles did, eight times? In "Nefertiti," they just kept playing the theme over and over. When that first showed up on a record it was revolutionary. You can play the head at two different speeds, or play it faster and faster, or as a fugue. You can make subtle adjustments in the dynamics.

After the head, there could be an interlude. Or you could take the last chord or the last couple of chords and let them be—just keep playing them as long as you want. Or we could do a little work, write some different chords or some background parts. We could imagine some chord changes that would follow the end of the theme—three chords, each lasting four bars, a short coda or interlude.

Mark: These things can be improvised, done on the spur of the moment. You don't have to work everything out in rehearsal, and you don't have to be bound by what you rehearsed.

Jazz Rehearsal is Different

Art: In our community, open improvisation is normal, but some people only make songs; they don't open up. They rehearse just to get the song down so they're not embarrassed on the gig. I think jazz rehearsal is different. We need to spend time working on the human aspects, the expressive and creative aspects of the music. We need to be in communication with one another, and that takes courage. We'll rehearse a tune for months and we'll try all the different things that I've been talking about, and then on the gig do none of them. Or, maybe something appears that we tried months ago. Rather than rehearsing to perfect something, you rehearse to be ready for everything. This is more like sports. You can't run your play exactly the way you designed it in practice because there's defense! You have to do off-shoots and variations. We don't do everything we prepared. If you do, that's show biz; it's not fresh.

If you listen to Weather Report, you can hear when they open. Sometimes they just party. The pianist Eric Deutsch will open up in the jam band context, but some kids have never heard that and don't know that it's allowed, or they're worried about commerce. They're afraid that if they don't do jazz properly, they won't be allowed to play at the jazz festival. They won't play music that confuses people about their stylistic identity, and they're afraid to take risks. This is where some of the kids are at in college. They want to be able to do something that is accepted in the community. They might be somewhat interested in learning their own language, but maybe even more compelling for some students is to be able to play a song, or sit in at a jam session playing standards, or play a Latin gig or a funk gig or a jazz gig or a classical gig and be able to do it well. There's nothing wrong with that, of course, but I prefer it when the music can open.

I remember the first time I heard the recording of Denny Zeitlin with Jerry Granelli and Charlie Haden playing "All the Things You Are." They got to the bridge and they played it about 14 times, and I thought, "That's really cool! I don't know whether that was planned or not." It just kept growing, and I thought, "Wow, is that going to be played again?" And then when the top of the form came back it felt amazing. You can try things a different way, and maybe that will reveal something beautiful or strange or fun.

There was a student here yesterday working on "Like Someone in Love," and I asked her to play the song in every meter, at every speed and in every style she could think of. The goal is to be able to sense it in all these different ways so you can go to the gig and set an environment that the piece has never lived in before, and that freshens it right away. It makes the piece sound totally different. It becomes a living thing rather than a reproduction from some record. Maybe it's never been played that way before, and maybe it will never be played like that again.

The word jazz means to me, "I dare you. Let's jump into the unknown."
     –Wayne Shorter (n.d.)

Below we suggest some additional areas of investigation, some of which fall squarely within the jazz tradition while others are more exploratory.

Six Choices About Motion and Tones

1. Tonality: linking with the established key, chords, and scales
2. Bi-tonality: playing in two different keys at the same time
3. Pan-tonality: playing outside of an established key center
4. Playing in the groove: linking with the established pulse and meter
5. Bi-rhythmic playing: different tempos or grooves played at the same time
6. Pan-rhythmic playing: waves, emotional gestures, sweeping phrases played out of time or out of synch with the other musicians

Art: A pianist called me up and said, "I'm teaching at a college and the students are so hip and talented I feel old fashioned and unable to play in their world. What could help me play with them?" What is a "modern" musician? I told him, with pitch there's tonality—fitting in with the chord or harmony that arises; there's bi-tonality—playing in two different keys at the same time; or pan-tonality—taking a 12-tone approach where all chromaticism and dissonance are fair game.

Similarly with rhythm, you can be in the rhythm of the others— playing in the pulse and the meter, subdividing in different ways. Or there are bi-rhythmic ways of playing—superimposing different speeds or meters that co-exist and sustain with the prevailing rhythm; or pan-rhythmic playing— here non-pulsing wave time, erratic motion, quickly shifting speeds, inflections, and accents are all fair game. If you are equally comfortable with all these points of view, you should be able to play with anyone.

Mark: Trying these different options means you need to find out what's alive in it for you. Otherwise, it's just a weird idea that Art had about playing in different rhythmic pulses or in different keys at the same time. You don't get the creative juice unless you're willing to live in those worlds and discover something for yourself.

Art: It's one thing to know about these options, and another to do the work to hear, execute, normalize, and manifest them in a group context. The question is: Are you willing to play what you actually hear? Or do you think, well, maybe somebody won't like it, or maybe I can't do It, or maybe it won't work, or it's not conventional in this kind of song or this situation, or maybe it'll be misunderstood.

I get accused of being a saboteur. "Are you trying to ruin my band or my workshop or my class?" I know I'm not doing any of that; I'm responding to what I sense and hear. We are constantly reinforcing our trust in what we hear and what we would like to play, and then we actually play it. I think it's important to make music with integrity. Music is about learning and growing. When people say, "Good show!" I think, this isn't a show. This is the way we are. This is how we actually play.

Conclusion

Go through the ear to the center
where sky is, where wind,
where silent knowing.
–Rumi (Barks, 2003, pg. 149)

When we bring love and awareness to the discipline of music making in the moment, and when we support others in doing the same, improvisation becomes a path of spiritual liberation. No philosophy, theory, or conceptual framework can capture this experience completely. We have to live it.

Improvisation is an investigation of what it means to be present and awake. This investigation is not about attaining a certain level of expertise or technical ability. Improvisation is about connection and community, and the path is available to everyone.

Art: Whether structured or not, improvisation is about playing the music that's singing in our hearts. It's about playing with people we love, whose presence we enjoy. Playing in unified bands for audiences who are present and listening, where the sound is good and the piano is excellent—this feels beautiful, uplifting, and mutually satisfying to all involved.

When a classroom becomes this kind of sanctuary, students get a taste of what the world of music making can be from the inside. Often that inspires them to learn, play, participate, and connect with themselves, with one another, and with the piece being created.

Living with gratitude, creativity, contact, a sense of purpose, joy, emotional journey, and focus in the present moment is a calling and a privilege. When we create an atmosphere of friendliness, relaxed awareness, aliveness, equality, and naturalness, we enjoy having our individual experiences as a group, listening and at times synching up in the deep quiet of silence or ecstatic release. This isn't about conceptual understanding; this is about living, embodying, and being music.

Afterword

The word jazz means to me, "I dare you. Let's jump into the
unknown."
–Wayne Shorter (n.d.)

The name of this book could easily be shortened to its essence—*Being*.
How to *be*, what it's like when we jump into being in the present
moment. Just being with what is occurring, or rather, just *being*. This
is not a static state, but dynamically fluid, constantly changing. And
there is no solitary, isolated being, but rather what Vietnamese Zen
master Thich Nhat Hanh calls "interbeing," the lively dance—
responding and expressing—to the world around us and to others who
are also dancing in our space.

I first came to know Mark Miller when he arrived decades ago as a
faculty member at Naropa Institute, in the Music department. His
shyness presents to the world modestly, behind a playful twinkle that
tells you he is deep and he is fun. His humor is wry, his powers of
observation stunning, and his heart wide open. It is when he picks up
his *shakuhachi* Zen flute or his silver flute or saxophone that he invites
me to be the music. It's impossible not to join him, dance in the notes,
respond to the sheer creativity of his expression. In our work together
over the decades at Naropa University, his natural presence, his
invitation to listen, his tenderness, and his collaborative curiosity have
enriched our little university with wisdom and skill.

It gradually becomes evident that Mark is a Zen practitioner not
because of any sense of religion or dogma, but because he is so
delightfully present. While he teaches lots of music courses at
Naropa—music theory, performance, improvisation, and studio—he

also teaches entering undergraduates a course in contemplative learning. There he coaches students to see, hear, feel the world around them and experience themselves as part of that world. He teaches them to be unafraid of themselves. He awakens them to the beauty of the ordinary.

Art Lande claims he isn't a meditator, but he could have fooled me. Forty years ago I heard Art perform with Bill Douglas and Paul McCandless, and I was swept into the enchantment of his intoxicating piano. He could play anything—genres of music, any beat or style. And he was pure magic. Years later, he took a part-time job assisting in my daughter's preschool, and I saw him enter a young child's world naturally, speaking her language, joining her in play. As Art says about improvisation: "We're like a bunch of four-year-olds. We just want to be with our friends, right? So, when you hit a note, I want to find it." With his uncanny quirkiness, he also knows how to *be* and how to be with others.

Together these two have generously shared the surprising, fresh world of jazz improvisation. But underlying the focus on music theory, minor and pentatonic scales, melody and harmony, and rhythm is the kind of lived wisdom that speaks to all of life. To *being*. How to be completely present with the constant flow of our experience. How to flow with one another, creating realms that beckon the listener to join in, awakening together.

There are many ways their work together, in music and in this book, resonate to the classical themes of contemplative practices, especially Buddhism. First is showing up—being present. The nakedness of improvisation requires such guts, walking a high wire without a net with other human beings, not sure where circumstances will take us. Developing an unbiased openness to whatever happens, with appreciation of our shared humanity.

Mark often speaks of how music requires us to step outside of conceptuality, just as meditation does. This non-conceptuality, however, is not blind stupidity because it's informed by a rich education in what's possible. Art observes, "You have to learn the rules, but music is not just about right and wrong. You have to practice being expressive and creative." In order to walk the high wire, we need to know what we are doing, and then we can explore what is possible. The truly adventurous are those who know the territory and possibilities, and then can play.

This requires that we allow our ambitions and emotions to drop away as we bring ourselves into the present moment with one another. As Mark writes, "The truth of the music (and of ourselves and our community) lies beyond our personal conception of what music ought to be. The point is to get to the music of this moment, and to the reality of our relationships, not to insist on the perfection of a particular vision or aesthetic. The point is to be open—not to the imaginary world that we think will fulfill all of our desires and expectations but to this world as it is, right here and now." This is how he teaches.

Knowing what's possible means opening to our sense perceptions, knowing personally, intimately, without labels the detail of our world. As Art remarks, "creativity is working with what actually happens," not about making something new. Mindfulness meditation or zazen attunes us to this moment, the symphony of fresh sensory experience presenting itself to us without fanfare. At Naropa, Mark teaches listening, attuning ourselves to the concerto of sounds that arise from street noise, voices in the next room, the clanking of pipes, and the subtle rhythm of breathings from a group. Only then do we pick up rudimentary instruments—cymbals, bells, whistles, tambourines—to appreciatively join the ensemble of ambient sound.

As Mark implies above, this kind of openness requires "pulling the plug on perfection." Spontaneity and naturalness have their own perfection that has nothing to do with our plans. They are based on what is, what the Buddhists call "things as they are" as opposed to what we think or want them to be. Things are often more beautiful when they are unfinished, surprising, asymmetrical, and humble. In Zen, this is called wabi-sabi, the beauty of the natural and uncontrived—and also of what's unexpected and fresh. Mark and Art speak of this as innocence, not trying, that invites much more play and possibility than what we think of as perfection.

But Mark doesn't claim that meditation and improvisation are the same thing. They overlap and share with each other. They are interrelated disciplines. He thinks of meditation as the way we practice on our own—"openness, awareness, and tenderness toward our experience." But improvisation is how we connect with others in a gesture of joy, responsiveness, and generosity. Mark writes, "In improvisation, we offer this experience to others, affirming our shared humanity through the fullness of our different points of view." Meditation can be solitary and personal. Improvisation connects with others while continuing to connect with our own experience. It's all about expression and response.

Isn't that our life? Tuning into ourselves fully while connecting with others? Together we recognize our fear of opening and being present, but so often the company of the other emboldens us to connect. If we dare together, we join the flow of what's happening, willing to ride the circumstances of the moment. Daring, spontaneity, trust, openness, and the joy of creativity—when we can wholeheartedly improvise in life, real adventure begins.

Fifty years ago when a young Sharon Salzberg, the renowned insight meditation teacher, was a college student she attended a talk by Naropa's founder, Tibetan meditation master, Chögyam Trungpa Rinpoche. She asked him for advice about where in India she should visit to learn meditation. He responded, "I think you had best follow the pretense of the accident." Isn't this dare what is asked of each of us? Jumping together into the unknown?

Acharya Judith Simmer-Brown, PhD

Acharya Judith Simmer-Brown, PhD, is Distinguished Professor of Contemplative and Religious Studies at Naropa University in Boulder, Colorado, where she has taught since 1978. She is an Acharya in the Shambhala lineage of Naropa's founder, Chögyam Trungpa Rinpoche.

Appendix: Meditation

Sitting is essentially a simplified space. It's not about some activity or about fixing something or accomplishing something. It's about ourselves…. If we don't simplify the situation the chance of taking a good look at ourselves is very small—because what we tend to look at isn't ourselves, but everything else.
  —Charlotte Joko Beck (1989, p. 17)

Meditation is an ancient practice with deep roots in Asian cultures and religions. In recent years, some of these traditions have migrated to the West, including Japanese, Vietnamese, and Korean Zen, Vipassana, and Tibetan Vajrayana Buddhism. New forms have emerged, including Shambhala Buddhism and Mindfulness Based Stress Reduction. These wisdom traditions and their Western offspring offer different philosophical frameworks and cosmologies, but basic meditation practice is very straightforward. Meditation is about taking time to get to know ourselves, to learn something about how our minds work and how our thinking and emotions influence our sense of who we are. According to Joko Beck (1989), when we take time to practice meditation, "we tend to see better what our lives are about and what needs to be done" (p. 17).

Before You Start, Stop

One of the most beloved meditation teachers is the Vietnamese Zen master, author, and poet, Thich Nhat Hanh (1998). He defines meditation as "stopping and looking deeply."

There is a story in Zen circles about a man and a horse. The horse is galloping quickly and it appears that the man on the horse is going somewhere important. Another man standing alongside the road, shouts, "Where are you going?" and the first man replies, "I don't know, ask the horse!" This is also our story.... We have to learn the art of stopping—stopping our thinking, our habit energies, our forgetfulness, the strong emotions that rule us (p. 24).

To practice meditation, stop what you're doing and find a place to sit quietly, somewhere you won't be distracted by family, friends, or social media. Sit comfortably in a chair or on a cushion. Allow your posture to be upright and awake, but not stiff or martial. Some people find it helpful to pay attention to a point of reference such as the breath, a word or phrase, or to listening as we did in Chapter 2. The idea is to be present with your breath or with listening, not to control or manipulate it. Sit comfortably and focus your attention on your point of reference. After a minute or two, your mind will inevitably wander as you begin to think about your day or your friends or your latest challenges and triumphs. When you notice this, begin again. Return your attention to your object of focus. That's it. That's the practice.

Thoughts and feelings will come up, but don't indulge them. In many traditions, part of the practice is to "label" thoughts and feelings as they arise. The point is to see that thinking and feeling are experiences that we have; they are not reality itself.

There is a big difference between thinking "I should be practicing music, not sitting here doing nothing" and labeling your thinking "I'm having the thought that I should be practicing music, not sitting here doing nothing." As the Vipassana meditation master Tara Brach teaches, you don't have to believe everything you think. Notice that thoughts are often constricting; they seem to make your world smaller. Notice that thoughts and feelings are transient; they come and go. When thinking becomes a distraction, acknowledge that, and return to your breath or to listening.

References

Akers, M., Dupre, J. (Directors). (2012). *Marina Abromović: The artist is present.* [DVD]. United States: HBO.

Anderson, J. (2020) Devotion to the unknown. Retrieved from http://joanandersonart.com/devotion_info.html

Bailey, D. (1993). *Improvisation: Its nature and practice in music.* Da Capo Press.

Barks, C. (2003). *Rumi: The Book of Love.* HarperCollins.

Beck, C. (1989). *Everyday Zen: Love and work.* HarperCollins.

Brach, T. (2003). *Radical acceptance: Embracing your life with the heart of a Buddha.* Bantam.

Brach, T. (2013). *True refuge: Finding peace and freedom in your own awakened heart.* Bantam.

Burns, K. (Director). (2001a). *Jazz: A film by Ken Burns.* Charlie Haden, performer. United States: PBS.

Burns, K. (Director). (2001b). *Jazz: A film by Ken Burns.* Wynton Marsalis, performer. United States: PBS.

Cage, J. (1961). *Silence: Lectures and writings by John Cage.* Wesleyan University Press.

Csikszentmihalyi, M. (1991). *Flow: The psychology of optimal experience.* Harper Perennial.

de Mille, A. (1991). *Martha: The life and work of Martha Graham.* Random House.

Eliot, T. (1967). *Selected Poems.* Harcourt Brace.

Ellington, D. (2013). Duke Ellington: "This isn't piano, this is dreaming" [Vimeo]. Retrieved from https://vimeo.com/55565898

Granelli, J. (n.d.) Private conversation with the author.

Grossenbacher, P. (2012). Mindfulness/awareness practice. [Presentation]. Public talk presented at Virginia Tech University, Blacksburg, VA.

Hanh, T. (1998). *The heart of the Buddha's teaching.* Broadway.

Johns, J. (2010). Jasper Johns. Retrieved from http://www.jasper-johns.org/jasper-johns-quotes.jsp

Koren, L. (1994). *Wabi-Sabi for artists, designers, poets & philosophers.* Stonebridge.

Krishnamurti, J. (1995). *The book of life: Daily meditations with Krishnamurti.* HarperCollins.

Lewis, G. (n.d.) Improvisation and the orchestra: A composer reflects. American Composers Orchestra. https://www.americancomposers.org/improvise/lewis_essay.htm

Mathieu, W. (1991). *The listening book.* Shambhala.

Mathieu, W. (1992). *Listening* [Presentation]. Public talk presented at Naropa University, Boulder, CO.

Otogawa, K. (1999). *Dharma talk* [Presentation]. Public talk presented at Naropa University, Boulder, CO.

Riedelsheimer, T. (Director). (2006). Touch the Sound [DVD]. Germany: Piffl Medien GmbH.

Rollins, S. (2015). The official Sonny Rollins page. Retrieved from https://www.facebook.com/offical sonnyrollins/?fref=ts

Rollins, S. (2016) *The pitchfork review.* Retrieved from http://pitchfork.com/features/from-the-pitchfork-review/9865-sonny-rollins-the-saxophone-colossus/

Shorter, Wayne, Wayne Shorter Quotes. (n.d.). BrainyQuote.com. Retrieved March 22, 2020, from BrainyQuote.com Web site: https://www.brainyquote.com/quotes/wayne_shorter_974421

Simmer-Brown, J. (1998). *Meditation practice* [Presentation]. Public talk presented at Naropa University, Boulder, CO.

Stevens, M. (2008). *Improvisation.* [Presentation]. Public performance presented at the third annual conference of the International Society for Improvised Music. University of Denver, Denver, CO.

Suzuki, S. (1999). *Branching streams flow in the darkness: Zen talks on the Sandokai.* University of California Press.

Suzuki, S. (1970). *Zen mind, beginner's mind: Informal talks on Zen meditation and practice.* Weatherhill.

Suzuki, S. (2012). Suzuki Roshi. Retrieved from http://suzukiroshi.sfzc.org/dharma- talks/tag/things-as-it-is/

Trungpa, C. (1991) *First thought, best thought: 108 poems by Chögyam Trungpa.* Shambhala.

Trungpa, C. (2005). *The myth of freedom.* Shambhala.

Welwood, J. (1979). Befriending emotion: Self-knowledge and transformation. *Journal of Transpersonal Psychology, 11(2),* 141–160.

Zen Peacemaker Organization. (2019). *The three tenets.* Retrieved from https://zenpeacemakers.org/the-three-tenets/

Index

About the Authors

Mark Miller

A saxophone, flute, and *shakuhachi* player, Mark Miller has toured and performed with a wide variety of improvising artists including Valerie Carter, Tuck and Patti, Paul McCandless, R. Carlos Nakai, Nawang Khechog, and Allen Ginsberg. His recordings include *World Without Cars* with Art Lande, named a top ten album of the year by Cadence Magazine, and the Grammy-nominated album *Illumination,* with pianist Peter Kater. A Zen practitioner for over 20 years, Mark is a Professor of Music at Naropa University, a leader in the international mindfulness movement. He views improvisation as a contemplative practice—an expression of individual presence and creative community. Mark holds an M.F.A. degree in jazz performance from California Institute of the Arts and currently lives in Boulder, Colorado with his wife, Dana Walker.

Art Lande

Art Lande is one of the most versatile and skilled improvisers in the world. As a Grammy-nominated pianist and composer, he has performed and recorded with many of the leading jazz musicians of the modern era including Joe Henderson, Bobby Hutcherson, Steve Swallow, Kenny Wheeler, Woody Shaw, Sheila Jordan, Jan Garbarek, David Liebman, Anthony Braxton, Randy and Michael Brecker, and Fred Hersch and Clark Terry, among others. His discography includes three recordings on the ECM label with *Rubisa Patrol*, critically acclaimed albums with Gary Peacock, Mark Isham, and Paul McCandless, and dozens of others. His solo piano recordings include *Hardball* (nominated for a Grammy Award), *The Eccentricities of Earl Dant*, and *Friday the Thirteenth* (the music of Thelonious Monk).

CPSIA information can be obtained
at www.ICGtesting.com
Printed in the USA
JSHW030813210920
7960JS00008B/75